125 BEST
Vegetarian
RECIPES

Byron Ayanoglu

WITH CONTRIBUTIONS FROM ALGIS KEMEZYS

Robert
ROSE

125 Best Vegetarian Recipes
Text copyright © 2004 Byron Ayanoglu
Photographs copyright © 2004 Robert Rose Inc.

For complete cataloguing information, see page 186.

Disclaimer

Design & Production: PageWave Graphics Inc.
Recipe Testing: Lesleigh Landry
Photography: Mark T. Shapiro
Food Styling: Kate Bush
Prop Styling: Charlene Erricson, Miriam Gee
Color Scans: Colour Technologies

Cover image: Mushroom-Spinach Lasagna with Goat Cheese (page 146)

The publisher and author wish to express their appreciation to the following suppliers of props
used in the food photography:

DISHES, LINENS AND ACCESSORIES
Country Floors, Toronto
En Provence, Toronto
Folly, Toronto
Muti Italian Country, Toronto
The Guild Shop, Toronto

We acknowledge the financial support of the Government of Canada through the Book Publishing Industry
Development Program (BPIDP) for our publishing activities.

Published by Robert Rose Inc.
120 Eglinton Avenue East, Suite 800, Toronto, Ontario, Canada M4P 1E2
Tel: (416) 322-6552; Fax: (416) 322-6936

Printed in Canada
1 2 3 4 5 6 7 8 9 10 FP 11 10 09 08 07 06 05 04 03

Contents

Acknowledgments

THESE RECIPES ARE DEDICATED TO THE LEGACY OF OUR MOTHERS, DESPINA AYANOGLU AND FREDA KEMEZYS

Special thanks to:
Aristedes Pasparakis; Jack Blum; Jonah, Chas, and Ralph Benmergui; Sharon Corder; Bob Dees; Charlotte Dix; Margaret Dragu; Wrenn Goodrum; Barbara Fitchette; Androula Haalbroom; Daniaile Jarry; Jon Kalina; Nathalie Kalina; Chef Lambrino (of Avli); Marion Lewis; Sharon and Peter Matthews; Soula Mbozi; Kamala McCarthy; Meenakshi; Amnon, Josh, Marion, and Ruth Medad; Anastasia Jarry-Mihalka; George Mihalka; Asher, Suzanne, and Paulette Motola; Leslie Orr; P.A. Super Marché (Montréal); Margie and Michael Pagliaro; Tom Rack; Juan Rodriguez; Martha Reilly; Judi Roe; Aziza Saleb; Leo Schipani; Carol Sherman; Jane, Kate, Jaimie, and Michael Sutherland; Cristallia Vassilyadou; Harry Xanthis; Wandee Young (of Young Thailand).

The New Vegetarian

❋ ❋ ❋

*The discovery of a new dish does more
for human happiness than the discovery of a star.*
— Jean Anthelme Brillat-Savarin

The olive tree is surely the richest tree of heaven.
— Thomas Jefferson

Vegetarian cookery is for everyone. It's what makes even everyday meals joyful and memorable. Color, texture, flavor, and infinite adaptability are just some of the extra benefits of non-meat edibles, rendering their healthful, low-calorie aspects almost a bonus. The recipes in this book will delight and nourish you, be they the substance of a vegetarian meal, or the supporting players of a meat-based spread.

Strict vegetarianism — and, by association, vegetable cookery — has been so politicised that it sometimes appears to have nothing to do with the kitchen and the dining table. For some people, vegetarianism is revered as a global panacea — the solution to every imaginable health problem, environmental concern, or political injustice. For others, it is anathema, the very word "vegetarian" an affront to their perceived First-World birthright to three "square" (read "meat") meals a day.

This controversy is hardly surprising when we consider the spotty history of vegetarianism in North America. In the 1950s, meat abstainers were viewed if not with outright suspicion, then at least with condescension. The alternate lifestylers of the 1960s changed all that, but at a price. As with all the other "inventions" of that most unusual decade, vegetarianism turned militant, intolerant, and holier-than-thou. And just to prove the point, sixties-type vegetarians developed intentionally dour recipes, based on misapplied, Japanese, macrobiotic philosophy — which is great for meditating on a serene mountain; not so great for surviving polluted, stressful urban environments.

And so this ludicrous polarity of vegetarians and their opponents — a situation of epic culinary fanaticism that confoundedly excludes both sides from the treasures and the unmitigated pleasures of lovingly prepared vegetables.

— ✣ ✣ ✣ —

For Mediterranean types like me — indeed, for anyone who was raised in the world's sunnier (if poorer) climes — vegetables, legumes and grains have no ideological connotations. They are simply the essence of everyday eating. During my formative years as a lower-middle class Greek in Istanbul, meat was a luxury, something reserved for Sundays and other holidays. Otherwise, we ate an extensive and highly inventive vegetarian diet, though we didn't know it as such. And even when small potions of meat did make their rare appearances, they were always accompanied by a slew of vegetable dishes. The North American standard of a 20-ounce steak, accompanied by a lonely potato and a watery salad, was something I encountered only when I first came to these shores.

Still, old habits are hard to kick. I've certainly eaten a lot of meat, poultry and fish over my last 38 years in the New World, but I've never lost my love for vegetables. I still cherish those that I ate from my mother's kitchen. In addition, my celebratory feasts now include the multitude of vegetable dishes I've tasted, recreated and adapted during three decades of travelling-to-eat, writing about food, and feeding thousands of happy customers in my various catering and restaurant businesses. Sample them for yourself. They just might change your ideas about vegetarian cooking forever.

Bon Appetit.

Byron Ayanoglu
Montréal, 2003

The Happy Vegetarian Kitchen

— ❈ ❈ ❈ —

At all times I strive to create food that is as nutritious as it is appealing. To succeed, I need to have fun in the kitchen. I'm a firm believer that "a happy chef is a good chef." Kitchen happiness, the key ingredient to eating happiness, depends on following a few, common sense rules.

Use a good frying pan on easy-to-regulate gas heat.
This is essential for the expedient sautéeing that browns/fries vegetables quickly, retaining their water (which makes them succulent and crunchy), while sealing into them the flavors of the oil and the condiments.

Use a hot, conventional oven.
I prefer a hot oven (400° to 425°F/200° to 210°C), rather than the more usual 350°F (180°C), for reasons of enhanced taste and texture. On the other hand, I never use microwave ovens (except for melting chocolate); despite the advantage of speed, I hate the texture and extreme heat that result from exposure to the microwave's electronic beam.

Cook attentively, not slavishly.
I've made a sincere effort to offer "exact" times for the different steps of the recipes. But let's be reasonable. Frying garlic for exactly 30 seconds (stopwatch and all) is not of the essence. Frying it for a short time and NOT burning it, is what it's all about. Keep in mind, too, that the timing of the garlic will also depend on the strength of your heat, and the conductive qualities of your pan: a cheap pan will get hotter in the middle and therefore requires more active stirring to prevent uneven cooking.

Planning to save time.
Even more than money, it is time that rules our most crucial decisions — especially when it comes to eating, which is predicated on hunger, the most impatient of our motivating urges. It is therefore essential to develop techniques that reduce the time needed for last-minute culinary operations.

— ❈ ❈ ❈ —

The greatest time saver of all is a little bit of planning and advance cooking. There are a number of essential preparations — from stocks to sauces to homemade crusts to pesto to reconstituted sun-dried tomatoes and rehydrated dried mushrooms — that live well in the fridge and/or freezer, and that give back buckets of happiness just for being ready to use, when you are ready to cook.

Timing the various steps of a complete meal in order to have everything ready more-or-less simultaneously is trickier to achieve, especially if working solo. In vegetarian dining we are helped quite a bit by the fact that many of the side courses actually benefit from being served lukewarm, giving them the chance to develop flavors, and giving us leeway to prepare them a little in advance, reserving "last minute" cooking for the main course, which should usually be served piping hot.

Timing is also served by following the French method for cooking vegetables: boiling them vigorously for 5 to 6 minutes, immersing them in ice-cold water, and draining them again to await their final enhancements and reheating. In short, half an hour of planning, chopping, boiling, draining and grating (all done to the beat of your favorite music), will make it a snap to pull the meal together at dinnertime, and allow everyone — even the cook — to enjoy it by making it look (and be) easy.

Make your dishes exuberant.
To be truly happy, a meal must "sing", both in the concocting and the presentation. Don't be bashful. Use the good things in profusion. Use fresh herbs in abundance. Use garlic as if it were going out of style (especially if cooked: it loses its raw pungency, but retains its benefits; no amount is ever too much). Use olive oil as unstintingly as your diet and/or sensibility will overlook. Oil is not of itself harmful. It becomes too acidic (and therefore hard to digest) in restaurant deep-fryers, where it's used to death, frying over and over again. In home cooking, used humanely and in moderation, it is the essence of great vegetarian cookery. The healthy human body needs a certain

amount of fat. A vegetarian diet, with its absence of animal fats, is incomplete without oil, and especially olive oil, the source of immeasurable eating pleasure.

Keep your meals in balance.

All diets need to be balanced if one is to remain healthy. It doesn't take a trained nutritionist to verify that an unbalanced diet will lead to loss of strength and vitality. A proper vegetarian diet must include a healthy dose of grains, beans and lentils, as well as a variety of vegetables (both roots and leaves), and yes, fats (like olive oil) in order to be complete. Far too many vegetarians of my acquaintance eat only what they like, and complement their diets with cheese, eggs and desserts. They pay the price with sallow complexions and low energy.

There is a lovely clean feeling that comes at the end of a vegetarian dinner — a striking contrast to the sense of bloatedness that so often accompanies the alternative. Let's enjoy that feeling, but let's also be sensible. And then we'll be truly happy.

Vegetarian Essentials

Many of the basic ingredients of fine vegetable cookery — from salt to olive oil to garam masala — have a long shelf life. Most of them are also prohibitively expensive when purchased in small quantities, and are often impossible to find except in specialized markets. It makes excellent sense (culinary and financial), to indulge in occasional shopping expeditions, and stock up as much as possible. Store your ingredients in a cool, dark place (or in your fridge or freezer), ready to have on hand when the fancy or the appetite strikes.
Here's my list of vegetarian essentials:

Stock

Homemade stock is the heart and soul (and body) of the best soups and sauces. In modern cooking, stock has the additional benefit of keeping fancy dishes within one's cholesterol and calorie reach, since it can replace some or all of the cream in those recipes.

It is therefore wise to have stock always on hand. This is easy, since the blessed substance lends itself to freezing without much loss in flavor or quality. And the best news of all is that making vegetable stock (as opposed to meat-based stocks) is amazingly mess-free and easy.

All it takes is 15 minutes of chopping and sautéeing, half an hour of unattended simmering, and then some grease-free straining. The whole affair is highly therapeutic, especially considering the delicious culinary benefits of ready-to-use, own-made stock. See my fuss-free recipes for Vegetable Stock (page 50) and Mushroom Stock (page 53).

Olive Oil

I revere and use it at every opportunity. I slather my toast with it, drizzle it over my pasta, salad and beans. It is even my preferred fat for sautéeing. And I've felt this way about it even before they discovered that instead of adding cholesterol to the diet, olive oil actually breaks it down and dissolves it. In fact, olive oil may be the only fun food that's good for you.

There is now a dazzling array of olive oils in all our markets. This is the natural consequence of the product's new-found popularity. Terms such as "extra virgin" and "cold-pressed" get rattled off at luncheons, usually followed by a long discussion on the relative merits of Luccan (Italian) versus Provençale (French). But the real cognoscenti discuss the clean taste of Spanish, the distinctive olive flavor of Portuguese, the upstart but acceptable Californian, and the intensely green-hued grandparent of them all, the olive oil of the many olive-grove laden regions of Greece.

An oil's "virginity" determines the amount of its olive flavor — and price. ("Extra virgin" refers to the very first pressing of the olives.) The flavor is even more intense if that first pressing was "cold", meaning that no heat was used in the extraction. Subsequent pressings, almost always heat-assisted, yield a golden oil, but with less flavor.

The wonderful, expensive flavor of cold-pressed virgin olive oil (especially if fresh: less than 6 months old) can be tasted only when the oil is eaten raw, and disappears once heated for cooking. Vegetable oil is perfectly suitable for high-heat operations like frying. With sautéeing, where the texture of olive oil is an asset, I choose a non-virgin (read, cheaper) variety. But when flavor matters — on salads or pasta, for example — I bring out my best and most aromatic oil.

VINEGARS

Newly rediscovered, vinegars have become the darlings of our most eclectic chefs. In truth, ounce for ounce, they contain more oomph and taste than most other condiments. And therein lies the pitfall: it's very easy to overdo vinegar. Even the correct amount, when used to sharpen a sauce or a glaze, must be cooked down first to chase out its acidity.

The most common use of red or white wine vinegars is still, as it always was, in salad dressings. Even here, it's best to use it sparingly, never more than 1 part vinegar to 4 parts oil. This is less true of balsamic vinegar (authentically produced only in Modena, Italy), which is sweet. Balsamic vinegar can even be used solo (if you are dieting, for example). In such cases, however, I prefer to use lemon: it's gentler.

Berry-flavored vinegars, like the phenomenally hyped raspberry and the lesser-known cassis (blackcurrant) varieties, can be deadly if misproportioned, clouding everything they dress in a mouthwash-like taste. In moderation, however, they can add an exotic touch to salads.

The subtle Chinese and Japanese rice wine vinegars have lovely uses, especially for tarting up Asiatic recipes, where European-style vinegars are far too overbearing. You can substitute ordinary white vinegar for these rice wine vinegars, but personally I avoid white vinegar (except for scrubbing my cutting board), just as I avoid microwave ovens and word processors. But don't get me started on those.

In any case, all vinegars are relatively inexpensive and they have a very long shelf life. I keep as many around as possible, so that I can properly mix and match taste sensations.

SPICES

They're all great, and they all have their uses, as long as they're quick-fried in the beginning of the cooking process to release their flavorful oils and to become digestible. There are a few exceptions to this rule, such as cinnamon inside a dessert, or the multi-flavored garam masala, which works as a garnish sprinkle; but generally, spices will not work to best advantage if they're just thrown onto a stew or a vegetable.

HERBS

My rule for herbs is simple: use them fresh, use them everywhere and use them in abundance. There is no flavor like theirs, and they're brimming with life-giving goodness.

TOMATOES

This wondrous fruit, second only to the marvellous bulb (garlic) in culinary popularity, has a thousand and one uses and comes in an equal number of varieties. Nothing will ever beat a fleshy, perfumed tomato, fresh from a late-August garden. But as life without tomatoes would be unbearable during the rest of the year, we must consider the alternatives.

Canned tomatoes: There's nothing wrong with canned tomatoes… much. They have little flavor, they're mushy, and they pick up metallic residue from the slightest bump on the can. Those canned in Italy have the best color, and are acidic enough to evoke the real thing.

Prepared tomato sauce: I don't have much use for the various grades of tomato "sauce" that line our supermarket shelves. They are loaded with additives and cost too much for what they are: diluted, flavored tomato paste.

Tomato paste: This is the one tomato byproduct that no amount of bad press can suppress. It has taken on its own identity, almost as though it were a separate ingredient from tomato, which it kind of is. It provides an indispensable background taste to many heirloom dishes. It is very acidic and I try to use it sparingly.

Sun-dried tomatoes: The concentrated tomato sensation I prefer is that of the sun-dried tomato — a landmark ingredient on the highway of modern cooking. Because it is naturally dried, and not boiled down like tomato paste, it's less acidic, and explosively tasty. Sun-dried tomatoes that are sold rehydrated in oil can be prohibitively expensive. The affordable way is to buy them dry; in this form, they keep for months, as long as they are stored in an airtight container in a cool, dark place.

To revive sun-dried tomatoes, take a handful at a time, soak them in some hot water for 30 minutes, drain them and add an equal measure of olive oil, then store them in the fridge. The oil itself becomes delicious for use as a condiment in salad dressings or on pasta. And by the way, since salt is a prime ingredient of sun-dried tomatoes (being the chemical agent that allows them to dry), the salt content of recipes using sun-dried should be scaled down accordingly.

The real thing: Nothing beats fresh, field-ripened tomatoes. The only kink to cooking with these is that they must be peeled and deseeded. The peel curls spikily during cooking and can offend the palate. As for the seeds, they annoyingly find their way into every crevice of the mouth.

The proper way to deal with tomatoes is to make a little slit on their smooth end, immerse them in boiling water for 30 seconds, and then fish them out with a slotted spoon. The peel slips off like a glove, taking the stem with it. The seeds and juice can then be prodded out of the ventricles either by finger or using a teaspoon. The flesh that remains is what is used for sauces and soups. The seeds can be strained from the juice and discarded. The juice can be reserved for sauces or soups.

Having said all that, I must admit that there are times when I'm just too rushed (or frazzled) to deal with peeling and deseeding mounds of tomatoes. What I do is wash the tomatoes, chop off their stems and then cut them into large chunks. This takes a bit longer to get the sauce going, but the advantage is that as the tomato begins to cook, its peel comes off; and since it is in only so many large pieces, I can fish it out with a spoon and proceed as if nothing has happened. As for the one piece of peel that always escapes and the seeds that inevitably distribute themselves all over the sauce — well, putting up with them becomes the punishment for my short-cut.

LEMONS

I've found so many uses for this delightful fruit that I once came close to owning a New York restaurant and calling it "Lemon." The complicated world of Manhattan leaseholds foiled my bid for the Abingdon Square premises of the proposed Lemon, so I never found out whether New Yorkers would have taken to the name.

The most lemony part of the lemon is its zest. This is the thin, yellow layer of its peel, which contains lemon oil, and adds sparkle to any recipe calling for lemon juice. The zest must be extracted before the lemon has been sliced or cut, and the only way to do it properly is with a lemon zester (wouldn't you know it?). A skinny instrument, invented by the French, it resembles a tiny set of brass knuckles mounted on a handle. It does its job by shaving off only the yellow zest without removing any of the bitter, white pith just underneath.

The zester creates lovely ribbons of fragile lemon essence which are wonderful in sauces. It is best to sauté them early in the process (usually along with the garlic), so that their flavor mellows during the rest of the cooking, and caresses rather than shocks the palate with its intensity. Oranges and even grapefruits can be zested with the same nifty instrument. A word about zested citrus fruits: all dehydrate quickly, having lost their outer skin. It is therefore necessary to juice the fruits soon after zesting. Use the juice in the recipe if it calls for it, or store it covered in the fridge or freezer for future use.

BEANS AND LENTILS

These are the best friends of vegetarians. They provide protein and satisfyingly rich textures, as well as a range of distinctively nutty, meaty flavors. In this book you'll find recipes for many varieties, including chickpeas, white and red kidney beans, and the pink, sweet-fleshed romano beans.

The only problem with beans is that they require planning and scheduling (what with overnight soaking followed by lengthy simmering), something that seems almost impossible in the normal course of our hectic, urban lives. Luckily (with few exceptions), canned, ready-cooked beans are perfectly acceptable for the recipes in this book.

A standard 19-oz (540 mL) can, once drained, provides 2 cups (500 mL) of beans. And draining is the key to their proper use. The water in which beans are packed has a residual metallic smell and (for me) an unpleasant taste. The solution is to drain them as soon as the can is opened, then wash them gently while tossing in a colander until they are completely rinsed of their canning liquid. Thereafter, remarkably enough, they taste of nothing but themselves.

Lentils (especially green lentils) are also available in cans; just wash them in the same way that you do for beans. However, lentils are easy to cook from scratch: they require no soaking, and cook up in about 30 minutes of simmering.

NUTS

A lot of the recipes in this book originate from sunny locations where nuts grow and, as a result, I use all kinds of them: pine nuts, cashews, pecans, walnuts, almonds and hazelnuts. I find all of them lend significant luxury and delicious crunch, as long as they're used judiciously — that is, not too many.

All nuts taste better if browned. Pine nuts, cashews and almonds, which can be purchased blanched (skinned) and pecans, whose skin is inoffensive, are best browned in a moderate oven for about 10 minutes. Make sure it's no longer — they burn easily — and that they're transferred to a dish immediately after the baking; otherwise, they will continue to cook on their own and burn.

Walnuts, being naturally drier, are best browned in a frying pan with a small amount of oil for 2 to 3 minutes.

Hazelnuts (or filberts), the most tasty of all nuts, are usually available only with skins on, and browning them involves an extra step, which is described in my recipe for Hazelnut Baklava (see recipe, page 176).

CHEESE

Gone are the days when we used to melt cheese indiscriminately over everything from nachos to broccoli. Our nutritionists have informed us that an excess of cheese is bad for our health — and the waistline, too. Nevertheless, there is no denying me a good Romano, Parmesan or Pecorino on my pasta. And bleak indeed would my life be without goat cheese.

Goat cheese: Imported or local, the relatively lean cheese of goat's milk is a supreme treat, especially when baked. It complements mushrooms, lettuce and eggplant. It sings under olive oil and freshly ground black pepper, and even turns pizza into a fancy dinner. Goat's milk cheese (or chèvre, as the French say) is as close to a food of the gods as humans can muster. Yes, it is expensive, but a little goes a long way.

Many southern European countries — including Portugal, Italy and Greece — make hard cheeses from goat's milk. Though all of them are wonderful, the ones I adore are the soft goat's milk cheeses that originate from France, and are copied rather successfully in North America. They have a soft, crumbly texture, a stark, deeply dairy flavor and a snow-white color. The originals from France normally have a tasty covering of mould or ash, whereas the domestic varieties are usually crustless, cost less and are straightforward. I eat the French chèvres on their own and use the North American equivalent for cooking.

Feta: My Greek birthright cheese appears several times throughout this book because it blends so wholesomely with so many of our favorite foods. Happily, it's not even necessary to be Greek to enjoy it. But here are a couple of Greek hints, concerning feta: every kind of feta should be gently washed, to remove some of the salt of the brine in which it is stored. If you want a completely saltless, very creamy feta, refrigerate it immersed in clean water after washing it. Drain again before using and get ready for a surprise.

For baking it is perfectly acceptable to use domestic feta, which is always less expensive than imported. But for salads, where authentic flavor is of the essence, you should choose something from the Balkans, especially Bulgaria and, of course, Greece.

Pastry crust

Just about any vegetarian dish, be it savory or sweet, takes on a wonderfully appetizing elegance when baked "en croûte." It looks great and it crunches just right. The trick is to use a crust that takes us away from the artery-clogging lard- and shortening-based crusts of our past.

To suit the times (and my palate), I favor an olive-oil-based crust (see recipe, page 116) for my savory pies; and I use the old Greek standby, phyllo dough, for my desserts.

The current popularity of phyllo is quite astounding to me, because it is tricky. It dries out very fast once out of its packaging, which means that one must work fast. It also needs a very dry surface, because moisture attacks it and makes it tear. Nevertheless, it is rewarding because it combines with butter to bake to a crisp airiness and complements whatever one wraps inside it.

Now, I also love a butter-based sweet crust, and here's one that was entrusted to me by Ruth Medad, the doyenne of patisserie. I don't offer any recipes that use it in the dessert section of this book, but I'd like to share this crust as an alternative to torte or pie shells for your favorites.

Ruth's Butter Crust

**MAKES
2 PIE CRUSTS**

Tips

You need not grease
your pie plate for
this dough: it is
buttery enough.

This dough freezes
with no loss, but
must be defrosted
completely in the
fridge (at least
24 hours) so that
it can be soft but
still cold.

10-INCH (25-CM) PIE PLATE, UNBUTTERED

2 cups	pastry flour	500 mL
½ cup	granulated sugar	125 mL
1 tbsp	baking powder	15 mL
7 oz	cold unsalted butter	200 g
2	eggs, beaten	2
Dash	vanilla	Dash
2 tbsp	pastry flour	25 mL

1. Put the 2 cups (500 mL) flour, sugar and
   baking powder in the bowl of a food processor.
   Cut butter in large chunks and add to the flour.
   Process at high for 1 to 2 minutes until mixture
   resembles coarse meal.

2. Add beaten eggs and vanilla. Process at high
   speed until blended. The mixture will already
   resemble dough, but still be a bit liquid. Add the
   2 tbsp (25 mL) flour and process at high speed
   until there is no more wetness on the sides of the
   bowl and the dough has shaped itself into a ball
   on the blades. Transfer dough to a dish, cover
   and refrigerate for about 1 hour to firm up.

3. Make the crust: Divide dough into 2 pieces and
   place one piece on the bottom of ungreased pie
   plate. Using your fingers, smooth out the dough
   to cover the bottom and sides of the plate.

4. To finish the pie: The crust need not be pre-
   baked but your filling should not be too wet.
   Since it can't be rolled out by rolling pin (it
   tears in transfer), you can top the pie with
   hand-shaped ribbons or other shapes, leaving
   some spots uncovered for a two-tone effect.

Appetizers

✤

Kopanisti (Feta Cheese Dip)

SERVES 4 TO 6

The most pleasant and mutually profitable kitchen collaboration I've ever had was with Chef Lambrino. Together, we designed the debut menu for Avli, his Greek eatery in Toronto. But when it came to the Greek meze (appetizer) dips, he was the undisputed master. I learned several of these wonderful dips, two of which are offered here, starting with this very easy cheese concoction — delicious served on toasted pita-points.

❋ ❋ ❋

Tip

This dip can be served immediately or it can wait, covered and unrefrigerated, for up to 2 hours. If refrigerated, let it come back to room temperature and give it a couple of stirs before serving.

1 tsp	olive oil	5 mL
¼ cup	minced green bell peppers	50 mL
¼ cup	minced red bell peppers	50 mL
8 oz	feta cheese, finely crumbled	250 g
1 tbsp	freshly squeezed lemon juice	15 mL
Pinch	paprika	Pinch
Pinch	hot pepper flakes	Pinch
¼ cup	extra virgin olive oil	50 mL
Pinch	dried oregano leaves	Pinch

1. In a small frying pan, heat 1 tsp (5 mL) oil on high heat for 30 seconds. Add green and red peppers and stir-fry for 2 minutes until softened. Take pan off heat and set aside.

2. In a bowl, combine feta and the sautéed peppers, mixing with a fork. Stir in lemon juice, paprika and hot pepper flakes.

3. Add olive oil in a steady stream to the feta-pepper mixture, continuously blending it in with a fork. When all the oil has been incorporated, the mixture should be airy, although somewhat gritty (from the feta crumbles). This is the correct texture; don't try to smooth it with a food processor or it'll turn into sludge.

4. Transfer the mixture to a serving bowl and garnish with oregano sprinkles.

Melizzano Despina
(Eggplant Dip #1)

SERVES 4

This simple eggplant dip is the one I grew up with. My mother, Despina, would whip it up at every festive opportunity to be served in conjunction with a slew of other vegetarian appetizers. It works wonderfully as a smoky-oniony dip for raw vegetables and also as a spread on sandwiches.

✖ ✖ ✖

Tip

This dip can be served immediately or it can wait, covered and unrefrigerated, for up to 2 hours. If refrigerated, let it come back to room temperature and give it a couple of stirs before serving.

PREHEAT OVEN TO 450°F (230°C)

1	medium eggplant (about 1 lb/500 g)	1
1 tsp	vegetable oil	5 mL
1	onion	1
2 tbsp	freshly squeezed lemon juice	25 mL
¼ cup	olive oil	50 mL
	Few sprigs fresh parsley, chopped	
	Salt and freshly ground black pepper to taste	

1. Brush eggplant lightly with vegetable oil. Using a fork, pierce the skin lightly at 1-inch (2.5 cm) intervals. Place on a baking sheet and bake for 1 hour, or until eggplant is very soft and the skin is dark brown and caved in.

2. Transfer eggplant to a working surface. Cut off 1 inch (2.5 cm) at the stem end and discard (this part never quite cooks through). Peel the eggplant by picking at an edge from the cut end, then pulling upward. The skin should come off easily in strips.

3. Cut the eggplant lengthwise and place each half with the interior facing you. With a spoon scoop out the tongues of seed-pods, leaving as much of the flesh as possible. To remove the additional seed-pods hiding inside, cut each piece of eggplant in half and repeat the deseeding procedure. Once deseeded, let cleaned eggplant flesh sit to shed some of its excess water.

4. Transfer drained eggplant flesh to a bowl. Using a wooden spoon, mash and then whip the pulp until smooth and very soft. Coarsely grate onion directly into the eggplant (the onion juice that results is very important to this dip). Add lemon juice and whip with a wooden spoon until perfectly integrated. Keep beating and add olive oil in a very thin stream; the result should be a frothy, light colored emulsion. Season to taste with salt and pepper. Transfer to a serving bowl and garnish with chopped parsley.

Melizzano Lambrino (Eggplant Dip #2)

VEGAN RECIPE

SERVES 4

Creamy and vibrantly flavored, this version of baked eggplant purée — and there are many, from Indian to Greek — is the most refreshing and memorable I know. A personal recipe from Chef Lambrino, this dip is great with toasted pita points or raw vegetables.

Tip

This dip can be served immediately or it can wait, covered and unrefrigerated, for up to 2 hours. If refrigerated, let it come back to room temperature and give it a couple of stirs before serving.

PREHEAT OVEN TO 450°F (230°C)

1	medium eggplant (about 1 lb/500 g)	1
1 tsp	vegetable oil	5 mL
1/2 cup	chopped onion	125 mL
1/4 cup	chopped fresh parsley, packed down	50 mL
1 tbsp	freshly squeezed lemon juice	15 mL
1 tsp	red wine vinegar	5 mL
1 tsp	Dijon mustard	5 mL
1/2 tsp	dried basil leaves	2 mL
1/2 tsp	dried oregano leaves	2 mL
2	cloves garlic, roughly chopped	2
1/4 cup	olive oil	50 mL
	Salt and freshly ground black pepper to taste	
1/4 cup	whole black olives (about 8)	50 mL

1. Brush eggplant lightly with vegetable oil. Using a fork, pierce the skin lightly at 1-inch (2.5 cm) intervals. Place on a baking sheet and bake for 1 hour, or until eggplant is very soft and the skin is dark brown and caved in.
2. Transfer eggplant to a working surface. Cut off 1 inch (2.5 cm) at the stem end and discard (this part never quite cooks through). Peel the eggplant by picking at an edge from the cut end, then pulling upward. The skin should come off easily in strips.
3. Cut the eggplant lengthwise and place each half with the interior facing you. With a spoon scoop out the tongues of seed-pods, leaving as much of the flesh as possible. To remove the additional seed-pods hiding inside, cut each piece of eggplant in half and repeat the deseeding procedure. Once deseeded, let cleaned eggplant sit to shed some of its excess water.

4. Put onions, parsley, lemon juice, vinegar, mustard, basil, oregano and garlic into the bowl of a food processor; process at medium and then at high speed, until ingredients are homogenized. With motor still running, add olive oil through feed tube in a very thin stream until emulsified.

5. Add deseeded eggplant flesh to the food processor; pulse on and off, just until incorporated. Transfer to a serving bowl, season to taste with salt and pepper, and garnish with black olives.

Baked Goat Cheese

A favorite item from my former New York-based catering company, La Grande Soiree, this recipe comes from my friend and partner, Wrenn Goodrum. She used to insist on the bitter radicchio leaves, but I find it just as wonderful on other greens, whether bitter (like endive or escaroles) or sweet (like the inner leaves of Romaine or Boston lettuce).

❊ ❊ ❊

Tip

This dish is great for parties, since it can be prepared in advance, stored in the refrigerator and baked at the last minute.

PREHEAT OVEN TO 400°F (200°C)
BAKING SHEET

4 oz	soft goat cheese, at room temperature	125 g
¼ cup	toasted pine nuts	50 mL
1 tbsp	drained green peppercorns	15 mL
12 to 14	small lettuce leaves (radicchio, Belgian endive, or inner leaves of Boston or Romaine lettuce)	12 to 14

1. In a bowl, combine goat cheese, pine nuts and green peppercorns; mix gently but thoroughly. Form cheese mixture into balls measuring about ¾ inch (2 cm). (You should end up with 12 to 14 balls.) Put them on a plate, cover loosely with waxed paper and refrigerate for at least 45 minutes to harden.

2. Place cheese balls on baking sheet, well spaced apart; bake in preheated oven for 4 to 5 minutes, until cheese is bubbling and has started to spread. Remove from oven.

3. Spread leaves of lettuce on a serving tray. Using a small spatula, remove baked cheese balls and carefully transfer each to the middle of a lettuce leaf. (The leaf acts as a platform for the cheese, and is eaten with it.) Serve immediately.

Goat Cheese Byzza

*Not being a devotee of
traditional pizza — for me
it's a last-resort food; the
kind of thing you order at
2 a.m. during an all-night
poker game — or even the
designer (read: expensive)
versions served at many
upscale restaurants, I came
up with this semi-eponymous
(BYron's piZZA = BYZZA)
creation. Quick and
entertaining, it works for
snacks, as well as the main
course of a casual dinner.
It employs a convenient
crust: A ready-made naan
(Indian flatbread) which
can be purchased wherever
East Indian foods are sold.
Byzza's only halfway difficult
step is the tomato sauce,
and even that is a snap
once you've mastered the
blanching-peeling-seeding
of fresh tomatoes.*

❋ ❋ ❋

Tip

Naan can be stored
frozen, ready to use
whenever that pizza urge
hits. In a pinch, you can
substitute the more widely
available pita bread.

PREHEAT OVEN TO 400°F (200°C)
BAKING SHEET, GREASED LIGHTLY WITH OIL

2	6-inch (15 cm) naan or pita breads, or pizza crusts	2
1 tbsp	olive oil	15 mL
¼ cup	Tomato Sauce (see recipe, page 138)	50 mL
¾ cup	shredded mozzarella cheese	175 mL
¼ cup	thinly sliced red onion	50 mL
¼ cup	thinly sliced green bell peppers	50 mL
1	small zucchini, thinly sliced	1
3 oz	soft goat cheese	90 g
	Few sprigs each of fresh parsley and basil, chopped	

1. Lightly brush both sides of the naan breads with olive oil and place on prepared baking sheet. Spread half of the tomato sauce evenly on each and sprinkle with mozzarella. Top with onion and pepper slices, then with zucchini slices.

2. Divide goat cheese into two equal portions and mold each into a patty measuring about 2 inches (5 cm) across. Place a cheese patty at the center of each Byzza.

3. Bake in preheated oven for 18 to 20 minutes until the underside of the crusts are crisp and the toppings have begun to char. Cut each Byzza into quarters and garnish with parsley and/or basil. Serve immediately.

Byzza Puttanesca

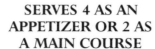

**SERVES 4 AS AN
APPETIZER OR 2 AS
A MAIN COURSE**

*Here's another variation on
my original Byzza — a
perky little number that
highlights the buttery
smoothness of fried eggplant
with tasty morsels like feta,
garlic and capers.*

✻ ✻ ✻

PREHEAT OVEN TO 400°F (200°C)
BAKING SHEET, GREASED LIGHTLY WITH OIL

½	medium eggplant	½
1 tsp	salt	5 mL
½ cup	all-purpose flour	125 mL
¼ cup	vegetable oil	50 mL
2	6-inch (15 cm) naan or pita breads, or pizza crusts	2
1 tbsp	olive oil	15 mL
¼ cup	crumbled feta cheese	50 mL
2 tbsp	chopped fresh mint or 1 tsp (5 mL) dried	25 mL
2 tbsp	chopped fresh parsley	25 mL
Pinch	dried oregano leaves	Pinch
2	green onions, finely chopped	2
1 tsp	drained capers	5 mL
3	black olives, pitted and chopped	3
3	cloves garlic, thinly sliced	3
Pinch	cayenne pepper	Pinch
1	small tomato, finely diced	1

1. Slice eggplant into rounds about ¼ inch (0.5 cm) thick. (You should get at least 8 slices.) Put in a bowl and add salt and cold water to cover. Let rest 5 to 10 minutes, then drain the eggplant slices and dredge them in the flour on both sides.

2. In a large frying pan, heat vegetable oil on high heat for 1 to 2 minutes, just until it's about to smoke. Fry first side of the dredged eggplant slices for 1 to 2 minutes; reduce heat to medium-high, turn eggplant over and fry another 2 to 3 minutes until the slices are soft and beginning to crust. Remove eggplant from pan and let them drain on a paper towel.

3. Lightly brush both sides of the naan breads with olive oil and place on prepared baking sheet. Top evenly with crumbled feta cheese, then with the mint, parsley, oregano and green onions. Arrange eggplant slices in single layer (about 4 per Byzza), then scatter capers, olive bits and garlic slices over the eggplant. Lightly dust each Byzza with a little cayenne.

4. Bake in preheated oven for 18 to 20 minutes until the bottom of the crusts are crisp. Remove from oven, cut into quarters and garnish with diced tomato. Serve immediately.

Potato Byzza

PREHEAT OVEN TO 400°F (200°C)
BAKING SHEET, GREASED LIGHTLY WITH OIL

1 lb	potatoes, unpeeled but well scrubbed (about 3)	500 g
2 tbsp	olive oil	25 mL
1/4 tsp	salt	2 mL
1/4 tsp	freshly ground black pepper	2 mL
2	cloves garlic, lightly crushed but not pressed	2
1/2 cup	sliced red onion	125 mL
2	6-inch (15 cm) naan or pita breads, or pizza crusts	2
1 tbsp	olive oil	15 mL
1	medium tomato, thinly sliced	1
1/2 tsp	dried oregano leaves	2 mL
3	cloves garlic, thinly sliced	3
6	black olives, pitted and chopped	6
2 oz	cheese, shaved (optional) Few sprigs fresh dill and/or rosemary, chopped	60 g

1. In a large saucepan, cover potatoes with plenty of water and bring to a boil. Cook for 5 minutes, then drain. Cut potatoes into neat 1/4-inch (0.5 cm) slices. Set aside.

2. In a large frying pan, heat 2 tbsp (25 mL) oil over medium heat. Add salt, pepper and garlic. Sauté 1 to 2 minutes until garlic browns. Remove garlic and discard. Add sliced onions and stir-fry for 1 minute.

3. Push onions to the sides of the pan and place in the middle the best-formed of your potato slices in a single layer. (Reserve any leftover slices for another use.) Reduce heat to low and cook about 50 minutes, turning every 10 minutes or so, until potatoes have browned and are soft when pierced. (The onions on the side will be reduced in volume and somewhat charred; discard any that have become too black.)

4. Lightly brush both sides of the naan breads with the oil and place on a baking sheet. Top with tomato slices, then sprinkle with oregano. Arrange potato slices to cover tomatoes, then top with cooked onions, garlic, olive bits and cheese shavings, if desired.

5. Bake in preheated oven for 18 to 20 minutes until the bottom of the crusts are crisp. Remove from oven, cut into quarters and garnish with the chopped herb(s). Serve immediately.

Goat Cheese Phyllo Nests with Cashews

SERVES 4

Phyllo is a magic ingredient. If properly deployed (oiled between each layer), it rewards with a festive look and is perfect for any party. Here, with the help of a muffin tin, we create frilly "nests" stuffed with a flavored goat cheese and topped with cashews.

✳ ✳ ✳

6 oz	softened goat cheese	175 g
2	eggs, beaten	2
¼ cup	chopped fresh parsley	50 mL
4	green olives, pitted and chopped	4
½ tsp	salt	2 mL
¼ tsp	freshly ground black pepper	1 mL
6	large sheets phyllo dough	6
¼ cup	olive oil	50 mL
16	roasted unsalted whole cashews (about 2 oz/60 g)	16

1. Mix goat cheese and eggs until combined but still lumpy. (There should be little bits of unmelted cheese in the mixture.) Stir in parsley, green olives, salt (use less, depending on the saltiness of the goat cheese) and pepper. Cover and refrigerate at least 30 minutes. (This will allow for easier handling.)

2. On a dry surface, layer 3 sheets of phyllo on top of one another, lightly brushing with olive oil between layers. Brush top surface with oil. Cut the layered phyllo into quarters. Carefully lift each quarter and gently fit into the middle of an oiled muffin cup, fluting the edges that rise off the cup to resemble a nest. Repeat layering-cutting-nest-building procedure with remaining 3 phyllo sheets to produce a total of 8 nests.

3. Spoon one-eighth of cheese mixture (about 2 tbsp/ 25 mL) into each nest. Top each with 2 cashews.

4. Bake in preheated oven undisturbed for 20 minutes or until phyllo is golden brown and the cheese filling has set. Remove from oven and let rest for 10 minutes. Unmold from the muffin tin (they'll slip off easily). Serve 2 nests per person.

Mint Feta Phyllo Nests

SERVES 4

In this variation on the previous recipe, we use less expensive feta with a minty twist. The sharp-tasting 3-to-1 ratio of feta to mozzarella can be mellowed by using equal portions (4 oz/125 g) of each cheese. And if you're using fresh mint (which we heartily recommend), feel free to double the quantity called for in the recipe.

✳ ✳ ✳

PREHEAT OVEN TO 350°F (180°C)
12-CUP MUFFIN TIN, 8 OF THE CUPS LIGHTLY OILED

6 oz	feta cheese, crumbled	175 g
½ cup	shredded mozzarella (about 2 oz/60 g)	125 mL
3 tbsp	minced red onion	45 mL
2 tbsp	minced red bell peppers	25 mL
1 tsp	olive oil	5 mL
Pinch	cayenne pepper	Pinch
¼ cup	chopped fresh mint (or 1 tbsp/15 mL dried)	50 mL
2	eggs, beaten	2
6	sheets phyllo dough	6
¼ cup	olive oil	50 mL

1. In a bowl, mash feta with mozzarella with a fork until well crumbled and mixed together. Set aside.

2. In a small nonstick saucepan, combine red onions, red peppers, 1 tsp (5 mL) olive oil and the cayenne pepper. Cook over medium-high heat, stirring, for 4 minutes or until softened but not browned. Remove from heat; stir into cheese mixture. Stir in mint and eggs until well mixed. Cover bowl and refrigerate at least 20 minutes or up to 24 hours.

3. On a dry surface, layer 3 sheets of phyllo on top of one another, lightly brushing with olive oil between layers. Brush top surface with oil. Cut the layered phyllo into quarters. Carefully lift each quarter and gently fit into the middle of an oiled muffin cup, fluting the edges that rise off the cup to resemble a nest. Repeat layering-cutting-nest-building procedure with remaining 3 phyllo sheets to produce a total of 8 nests.

4. Spoon one-eighth of cheese mixture (about 3 tbsp/ 45 mL) into each nest.

5. Bake in preheated oven undisturbed for 20 minutes or until phyllo is golden brown and the cheese filling has set. Remove from oven and let rest for 10 minutes. Unmold from the muffin tin (they'll slip off easily). Serve 2 nests per person.

Individual Asparagus and Goat Cheese Flan

SERVES 4

Asparagus is the most elegant of vegetables and, happily for us, it is available year-round. In the south of France, where they only eat it in season (spring), they make a delicious omelette with the thinnest stalks.

Here's a take on their omelettes which works with any size asparagus you can find. It ends up saucy and tart — a perfect appetizer for a dinner party.

PREHEAT OVEN TO 400°F (200°C)
FOUR ½-CUP (125 mL) RAMEKINS
BAKING SHEET

1 lb	asparagus, bottom 1½ inches (4 cm) trimmed (about 24 stems)	500 g
4 oz	softened goat cheese	125 g
2	eggs, beaten	2
2	green onions, chopped into ¼-inch (0.5 cm) pieces	2
1 tbsp	freshly squeezed lemon juice	15 mL
¼ tsp	salt	1 mL
¼ tsp	freshly ground black pepper	1 mL
1 tsp	olive oil	5 mL
2 tbsp	pine nuts	25 mL

1. Bring a large pot of water to a boil. Add trimmed asparagus, return to a boil and cook for 3 minutes. Drain. Rinse under cold water; drain. Cut into 1½-inch (4 cm) pieces; set aside.

2. In a bowl, mix goat cheese with eggs until combined but still lumpy. Stir in asparagus, green onions, lemon juice, salt and pepper. Brush bottom of ramekins with oil. Divide asparagus mixture between ramekins; sprinkle evenly with pine nuts.

3. Transfer ramekins to baking sheet. Bake in preheated oven for 15 to 18 minutes or until set around edges but still slightly runny just at the center. Do not unmold. Serve immediately in ramekins.

Potato Byzza (page 28)

Fried Zucchini

SERVES 4 AS AN APPETIZER OR SIDE VEGETABLE

This is a big favorite in Greece, where it is always accompanied by Tzatziki. Its appeal lies in the flavorful, still-crunchy zucchini — and, of course, the sinful pleasure that accompanies all fried foods. Fortunately, it is a relatively benign fried item, in that it doesn't absorb much oil — at least, not nearly as much as fried eggplant, which is often served alongside it.

❈ ❈ ❈

12 oz	zucchini (about 2 medium)	375 g
1 cup	all-purpose flour	250 mL
1/4 tsp	salt	2 mL
1/4 tsp	freshly ground black pepper	2 mL
1/2 cup	vegetable oil	50 mL
1 cup	Tzatziki Sauce (see recipe, page 166) or	250 mL
4	lemon wedges	4

1. Trim stems of the zucchini. Slice lengthwise on the diagonal, about 1/4 inch (0.5 cm) thick, to obtain long, thin, elegant slices. Put in a bowl and add cold water to cover; let soak.

2. In another bowl, sift together flour, salt and pepper. Place this bowl near the stove, along with the bowl containing the zucchini slices.

3. In a large frying pan, heat oil over medium-high heat until it's just about to smoke. Working quickly, take a zucchini slice from the water, dredge thoroughly in the seasoned flour, and then put it into the hot oil. Repeat procedure until the pan is filled with a single layer of zucchini slices. Fry the slices for 2 minutes on one side until golden brown, but not burned; turn them over, using tongs if possible, and fry another 2 minutes.

4. Transfer the fried zucchini slices to a plate lined with a paper towel, then repeat dredging/frying procedure with any remaining slices. Once cooked, transfer all the zucchini slices to a plate. Serve immediately, accompanied by Tzatziki Sauce or lemon wedges.

Mint Feta Phyllo Nests (page 31)

Zucchini Croquettes with Yogurt Salad

MAKES 48 CROQUETTES, SERVING 8

Notwithstanding the army of nutritional zealots apparently bent on eliminating it from our diets, deep-fried food is still the number-one party favorite. This particular item — juicy and flavorful on the inside, crispy and crunchy on the outside — is not without virtue, however: It absorbs very little oil and is composed primarily of shredded zucchini, a very healthy vegetable. It was always a hit at my mother's feast-day buffets in Istanbul, and has continued to play a significant role in my own holiday entertaining. The yogurt salad that accompanies the croquettes can be enjoyed with a number of other dishes — essentially, anything that benefits from a refreshing side course.

✳ ✳ ✳

Yogurt Salad

1 cup	yogurt	250 mL
1	2-inch (5 cm) piece English cucumber, finely diced	1
2	green onions, finely chopped	2
1	medium tomato, seeded and finely diced	1
½ tsp	salt	2 mL
½ tsp	cayenne pepper	2 mL
1 tbsp	freshly squeezed lemon juice	15 mL
1 tsp	extra virgin olive oil	5 mL

Zucchini Croquettes

1 lb	zucchini (about 3 medium)	500 g
¼ cup	chopped fresh mint or dill	50 mL
½ cup	all-purpose flour	125 mL
1 tsp	salt	5 mL
1 tsp	freshly ground black pepper	5 mL
½ tsp	ground nutmeg	2 mL
4 oz	sharp cheese, shredded (such as Pecorino, Crotonese or old Cheddar)	125 g
2	eggs, beaten	2
2 to 3 cups	vegetable oil	500 to 750 mL

1. **Yogurt Salad:** In a bowl, stir together yogurt, cucumber, green onions, tomato, salt and cayenne. Add lemon juice and olive oil; mix well. If using soon, cover and save unrefrigerated. If not, refrigerate (up to several hours), but let come to room temperature before serving.

2. **Zucchini Croquettes:** In another bowl, shred zucchini through the largest holes of a grater. Stir in mint. Sift flour into bowl and mix in. Stir in salt, pepper, nutmeg and cheese. Add eggs and fold-mix just until all the liquid appears to be absorbed.

3. In a large pot or wok, add vegetable oil to a depth of 1 inch (2.5 cm). Heat to 325°F (160°C) on a deep-fry thermometer. (If you don't have a thermometer, heat oil over medium-high heat; test by adding a bit of croquette batter: it should sizzle and rise.) Add croquette batter in 2 tbsp (25 mL) dollops; add as many as the pot can accommodate without them touching one another. Fry 2 minutes per side or until crisp and browned. Drain on paper towels. Repeat procedure with remaining batter.

4. It is best to set out the yogurt sauce and let guests eat the croquettes as soon as they are cooked, with spoonfuls of the yogurt on the side. If you must fry them all before serving, keep the early batches warm in a low oven and serve as soon as the last ones are ready.

Olive Oil Crostini

MAKES 70 CANAPÉS

For my pie recipes, I created a special olive oil crust which also works wonderfully well for canapés. It's simple: Just bake the little rounds of crust with any topping you like — or use the one presented here.

Tip

The crusts can also be baked plain (with only egg wash on them) for 18 to 22 minutes at 400°F (200°C), until golden brown. Allow them to cool and then dress them with any cold topping you choose. They provide a lush, homemade alternative to store-bought crackers and biscuits.

PREHEAT OVEN TO 400°F (200°C)
BAKING SHEET, LIGHTLY GREASED WITH VEGETABLE OIL

4	sheets Olive Oil Crust (see recipe, page 116)	4
1	egg	1
1 tbsp	milk	15 mL
2	medium tomatoes, finely diced	2
6 to 8	black olives, pitted and chopped	6 to 8
1 tsp	dried oregano leaves	5 mL
1 1⁄2 cups	coarsely grated Pecorino or Parmesan cheese	375 mL
1⁄2 cup	thinly sliced red onion	125 mL
	Few sprigs fresh parsley, chopped	

1. On a floured surface, lay out the sheets of olive oil crust and, using a small glass or cookie cutter, cut out circles 1 1⁄2 inch (4 cm) in diameter. (The circles will shrink a little when they're cut.) Transfer them to prepared baking sheet, spacing them slightly apart.
2. Reshape the trimmings of leftover dough, flour on both sides and roll out to 1⁄8 inch (0.25 cm) thickness. Cut out additional circles and transfer them to the cookie sheet. (You should end up with about 70 rounds.)
3. Whisk together egg and milk; brush over the rounds of dough. Top each with some diced tomato, chopped olive, a sprinkle of oregano, a little cheese and a few thin slices of onion. (Don't worry if ingredients fall between the biscuits: you'll be able to cut them off later.)
4. Bake rounds in preheated oven for 18 to 20 minutes, until the bottom of the crusts have browned and the onions are beginning to char. Using a spatula, remove the crostini from the baking sheet. Trim any overhanging ingredients and transfer the crostini to a presentation plate. Garnish with chopped parsley and serve as soon as possible.

Braised Endive and Tomato Gratinée

SERVES 2

Endive is plentiful and available throughout the year. Here's a recipe that combines endive with sunbelt flavors and uses the ancient French culinary method of braising or slow cooking.

2	medium endives	2
2 tbsp	water	25 mL
1 tbsp	olive oil	15 mL
4	black olives, pitted and cut into thirds	4
2	cloves garlic, thinly sliced	2
2	sun-dried tomatoes, cut into thirds	2
1	ripe tomato, cut into $\frac{1}{2}$-inch (1 cm) wedges	1
Pinch	dried oregano leaves	Pinch
Pinch	dried basil leaves	Pinch
$\frac{1}{4}$ tsp	salt	1 mL
$\frac{1}{8}$ tsp	freshly ground black pepper	0.5 mL
2 oz	sharp cheese, shredded (such as Pecorino, Parmesan or old Cheddar)	60 g
	Few sprigs fresh basil or parsley, chopped	

1. Place endives into a small shallow pot with a lid. Add water, olive oil, olives, garlic, sun-dried tomatoes, tomato, oregano, basil, salt and pepper; cook over high heat for 1 to 2 minutes or until bubbling. Push the tomato wedges to the bottom of the pot around the endives, pushing the other ingredients into the ensuing liquid. Reduce heat to minimum, cover and cook undisturbed for 35 minutes or until soft and pierceable. (The recipe can prepared to this point up to 2 hours in advance.)
2. Carefully transfer endives to a small ovenproof dish. (They should fit snugly.) Cover endives with sauce. With a sharp knife, slice the endives halfway down and open up the cuts so that they are somewhat butterflied. Sprinkle shredded cheese evenly on the butterflied surfaces. Place under a hot broiler for 3 to 4 minutes, until the cheese is bubbling and beginning to char. Lift the endives carefully with a spatula onto 2 plates and pour sauce around them. Garnish with chopped basil or parsley. Serve immediately.

Mini Savory Crêpes

SERVES 6 TO 8

Here's a crêpe recipe adapted from the dessert crêpes I learned to love in the beautiful countryside outside Montreal, where they are served in oodles of warm maple syrup. This savory version makes for a beautiful sit-down starter if served face up and an equally good stand-up hors d'oeuvre if rolled.

❋ ❋ ❋

Tip

To make the crêpes sweet, simply omit the salt, onion, red pepper and black pepper from this recipe, and fry them in butter instead of oil.

PREHEAT OVEN TO 200°F (100°C)

1 cup	all-purpose flour	250 mL
1 tsp	baking powder	5 mL
½ tsp	salt	2 mL
2 tbsp	freshly squeezed lemon juice	25 mL
2	eggs, beaten	2
1¼ cups	milk	300 mL
¼ cup	finely diced red onion	50 mL
¼ cup	finely diced red or green bell peppers	50 mL
½ tsp	freshly ground black pepper	2 mL
¼ to ½ cup	olive oil	50 to 125 mL
2	red bell peppers, roasted, skinned and sliced into ¼-inch (0.5 cm) ribbons	2
½ cup	sour cream or yogurt	125 mL

1. Sift flour into a working bowl, then sprinkle with baking powder and salt. Sprinkle lemon juice on the baking powder (you'll see it foam). Add beaten eggs and milk all at once and whisk just until well blended and the mixture has the consistency of heavy cream. Do not overbeat — some little undissolved lumps are desirable — otherwise, the crêpes will be rubbery when cooked. Let the mixture rest for about 10 minutes.

2. Stir in red onions, red and green peppers and black pepper.

3. In a large frying pan or on a griddle at medium-high heat, add just enough oil to grease the surface. With a measuring cup or spoon, pour the batter in 2 tbsp (25 mL) amounts onto the cooking surface, allowing enough space between them for expansion. This quantity of batter will make pancakes measuring about 3 inches (8 cm) in diameter.

4. Fry the crêpes until deep bubbles begin to appear on the top surface, about 2 minutes; flip them over and fry another 1 to 2 minutes, until lightly browned. Remove from the pan and brush both sides of each crêpe with olive oil. Re-grease the pan and, using the same procedure, cook remaining crêpes in batches. Cooked crêpes can be kept warm in a low oven, until the rest are fried. Exactly how much oil you use depends on how generously you grease the pan and brush the pancakes.

5. When all the pancakes have been fried (you'll get about 24), garnish with ribbons of roasted skinned red pepper and a little sour cream. Serve as soon as possible, open-faced or rolled.

Tortilla Espagnola (Potato Omelette)

SERVES 4 FOR BRUNCH OR AS AN APPETIZER; 8 TO 16 AS AN HORS D'OEUVRE

Here's a dish that, more often than not, totally escapes the North American culinary understanding. Admittedly, a cold omelette made with more potato than egg sounds just about as gourmet as leftover pizza. And yet, all over its native Spain this tortilla is eagerly sought after in tapas bars and restaurants.

❋ ❋ ❋

Tip
The taste-trick is to include serious quantities of aromatics when frying the potatoes and to use some sharp cheese for the topping.

1 lb	potatoes, unpeeled but well scrubbed (about 3)	500 g
1/4 cup	olive oil	50 mL
1/2 tsp	salt	2 mL
1/2 tsp	freshly ground black pepper	2 mL
1	onion, thinly sliced	1
1/2	red bell pepper, thinly sliced	1/2
5	eggs	5
2 tbsp	water	25 mL
1 tbsp	all-purpose flour	15 mL
1/2 tsp	paprika	2 mL
4	cloves garlic, thinly sliced	4
1/2 tsp	dried oregano leaves	2 mL
1/2 cup	grated mozzarella	125 mL
1/2 cup	grated sharp Cheddar	125 mL
	Hot Olive Oil (see recipe, page 160)	

1. In a large saucepan over high heat, boil potatoes for 6 to 7 minutes until pierced easily with a fork, but not in the least crumbling. Drain and let cool. Cut potatoes in half lengthwise, then cut crosswise into thin half-rounds, about 1/4 inch (0.5 cm) thick. Set aside.

2. In a large ovenproof frying pan, heat oil over medium heat for 1 minute. Add salt and pepper and stir. Add sliced potatoes, onion and red pepper; sauté for 10 to 12 minutes, turning frequently, until they are browned, but not burnt.

3. Meanwhile, preheat the broiler and beat together the eggs, water, flour and paprika in a small bowl.

4. Add sliced garlic and oregano to the frying pan and toss actively for 1 minute to fry the garlic slightly. Pour egg mixture over vegetables and shake the pan to distribute evenly. Let cook for 1 minute until eggs start to set. Sprinkle omelette evenly with the cheeses and let cook for another 3 minutes. Place under a broiler for 2 minutes to melt the cheese completely and to finish setting the eggs. Remove from broiler and let rest for 2 minutes.

5. To serve, slide the omelette off the pan onto a plate. (It will look like a flat cake — ergo, "tortilla.") Cut into quarters, eighths or sixteenths. Serve with Hot Olive Oil, to be added to taste at table.

Asian Spring Rolls

VEGAN RECIPE

MAKES ABOUT 20 ROLLS

Deep-fried treats like these — with their attendant calorie-guilt, and potential for oily mess — I reserve for parties and other special occasions. They work well as passed hors d'oeuvre for stand-up parties and just as well on a buffet. Here are two recipes, starting with this personal version of an Asian-style spring roll, to celebrate the continent of its origin.

Tips

Spring rolls can be prepared and assembled early in the day. Keep covered in the refrigerator until ready to fry but let come back to room temperature before proceeding.

If you can't find large spring roll skins, use 40 of the more readily available 5-inch (12 cm) egg roll wrappers, and use half as much filling per wrapper.

4 oz	glass noodles (or mung bean thread noodles)	125 g
1/2 cup	vegetable oil	125 mL
2 tbsp	minced garlic	25 mL
2 tbsp	minced gingerroot	25 mL
1/2 tsp	freshly ground black pepper	2 mL
2	onions, thinly sliced	2
1 1/2 cups	grated cabbage, packed down	375 mL
1/4 cup	soy sauce	50 mL
2 tbsp	granulated sugar	25 mL
1 1/2 cups	grated carrots, packed down	375 mL
6	green onions, cut into 1/2-inch (1 cm) pieces	6
2 cups	bean sprouts	500 mL
20	large (9-inch/22.5 cm square) spring roll skins (see Tips, left)	20
1 tbsp	all-purpose flour	15 mL
2 tbsp	water	25 mL
2 1/2 cups	vegetable oil (for deep-frying), approx.	625 mL
	Few sprigs fresh coriander, chopped	
	Asian Hot Oil (see recipe, page 160)	

1. Soak the glass noodles in cold water to cover for at least 30 minutes.
2. Make the filling: In a wok or large frying pan, heat 1/2 cup (125 mL) oil on high heat for 1 minute. Add garlic, ginger and pepper and stir-fry for 30 seconds. Add the sliced onions and stir-fry for 1 minute. Add the grated cabbage and stir-fry for 1 minute. Add soy sauce and sugar and stir-fry for 30 seconds.
3. Drain glass noodles well and add to the wok; reduce heat to medium-high and stir-fry actively for 1 to 2 minutes until noodles are moistened and light brown in color. Add carrots and green onions; stir-fry actively for 2 minutes, mixing everything as much as possible. Add bean sprouts and stir-fry for 30 seconds.

4. Place a colander over a large mixing bowl; quickly transfer the stir-fried ingredients to the colander, cover and let the mixture rest, unrefrigerated, for at least 2 hours to drain its excess oil. (You needn't press on the mixture; it'll drain by itself.) Once drained, transfer the mixture to a fresh bowl and mix the ingredients by hand, pulling the noodles apart as you go.

5. Assemble the spring rolls: On a dry surface, spread out one of the egg roll skins so that a corner is facing you. Put $\frac{1}{4}$ cup (50 mL) of the filling 2 inches (5 cm) in from the corner. Fold the corner over the filling and tuck to tighten. Roll once. Fold in the two corners on each end of the roll, as if making an envelope. Roll up the spring roll, until only the farthest corner from you is left unrolled. Dissolve flour in water; spread a little flour paste on the corner, and stick it down. Your finished spring roll should be about 3 inches (7.5 cm) long and about 1 inch (2.5 cm) wide. Repeat procedure with remaining skins until all the filling has been used. (You should get about 20 spring rolls.)

6. In a frying pan or deep-fryer, heat a sufficient quantity of oil to cover the spring rolls over high heat. Fry the spring rolls in batches until golden but not brown, transferring them when done to drain on a paper towel. (Keep in mind that spring rolls fry very fast and will need to be turned frequently.) With a sharp knife, cut each roll diagonally into two halves. Present them on a platter garnished with chopped coriander and a little dipping bowl of hot oil.

Wild Spring Rolls

MAKES ABOUT 20 ROLLS

Here's a spring roll that owes nothing but its skin to Asia, and can thus work with a variety of other items — such as you might find in a buffet of international cuisine. The wild mushrooms used here can be portobello, shiitake or oyster, or a combination of all three. In a pinch, you can use ordinary mushrooms, although at the expense of considerable "wildness."

✻ ✻ ✻

Tips

Prepare wild rice by boiling over medium heat for 50 to 60 minutes, until the grain husks split to reveal the white interior and their texture is al dente; drain and reserve. Use about 7 oz (200 g) of raw wild rice to get 3 cups (750 mL) of cooked rice.

If you can't find large spring roll skins, use 40 of the more readily available 5-inch (12 cm) egg roll wrappers, and use half as much filling per wrapper.

¼ cup	olive oil	125 mL
½ tsp	salt	2 mL
½ tsp	freshly ground black pepper	2 mL
2	onions, finely diced	2
5 cups	finely sliced wild mushrooms	1.25 L
5	cloves garlic, finely chopped	5
½ cup	walnut bits	125 mL
10	sun-dried tomatoes, soaked, drained and cut into thin ribbons	10
3 cups	cooked wild rice (see Tips, left)	750 mL
¼ cup	finely chopped fresh parsley	50 mL
20	large (9-inch/22.5 cm square) spring roll skins (see Tips, left)	20
1 tbsp	all-purpose flour	15 mL
2 tbsp	water	25 mL
2½ cups	vegetable oil (for deep-frying), approx.	625 mL
1 cup	Tomato Sauce, warmed (see recipe, page 138)	250 mL

1. Make the filling: In a large frying pan, heat olive oil on high heat for 1 minute and stir in salt and pepper. Add onions and stir-fry for 2 to 3 minutes until soft. Add sliced mushrooms and stir-fry for 3 to 4 minutes until softened. Add garlic and walnut bits and stir-fry for 2 minutes.

2. Immediately transfer mixture to a bowl and add the thin ribbons of sun-dried tomatoes. Add the cooked wild rice and stir until well mixed. Add chopped parsley and mix to distribute evenly. Cover mixture and let rest 1 to 2 hours, unrefrigerated.

3. Assemble the spring rolls: On a dry surface spread out one of the egg roll skins so that a corner is facing you. Put ¼ cup (50 mL) of the filling 2 inches (5 cm) in from the corner. Fold the corner over the filling and tuck to tighten. Roll once. Fold in the two corners on each end of the roll, as if making an envelope. Roll up the spring roll, until only the farthest corner from you is left unrolled. Dissolve flour in water; spread a little flour paste on the

Spring rolls can be prepared and assembled early in the day. Keep covered in the refrigerator until ready to fry, but let come back to room temperature before proceeding.

corner, and stick it down. Your finished spring roll should be about 3 inches (7.5 cm) long and about 1 inch (2.5 cm) wide. Repeat procedure with remaining skins until all the filling has been used. (You should get about 20 spring rolls.)

4. In a frying pan or deep-fryer, heat a sufficient quantity of oil to cover the spring rolls over high heat. Fry the spring rolls in batches until golden but not brown, transferring them when done to drain on a paper towel. (Keep in mind that spring rolls fry very fast and will need to be turned frequently.) With a sharp knife, cut each roll diagonally into two halves. Present them on a platter with a small dipping bowl of tomato sauce.

Quesadilla

**SERVES 4 AS A MAIN
COURSE; UP TO 16 AS
AN HORS D'OEUVRE**

*This spirited flavor
combination from south of
the border will spark up a
bleak winter evening as easily
as it accents a sparkling
summer's lunch in the garden.
It's a simple combination of
tomato sauce, refried beans
and cheese that's sandwiched
between tortillas and fried.
You can use 1 tbsp (15 mL)
oil for large quesadilla, as
suggested here, but you'll
achieve a crisper, more
appealing texture (especially
for kids) if you double that
amount. Up to you.*

2 cups	cooked red kidney beans	500 mL
2 tbsp	lime juice	25 mL
4	cloves garlic, roughly chopped	4
1 tbsp	vegetable oil	15 mL
½ tsp	salt	2 mL
½ tsp	freshly ground black pepper	2 mL
1 tsp	whole cumin seeds	5 mL
Pinch	ground cinnamon	Pinch
8	large (9-inch/22 cm) flour or corn tortillas	8
½ cup	Tomato Sauce (see recipe, page 138) or store-bought	125 mL
1 to 1½ cups	grated cheese (mozzarella, Monterey Jack, Cheddar or Parmesan)	250 to 375 mL
¼ to ½ cup	vegetable oil	50 to 125 mL
	Few sprigs fresh coriander, chopped	
	Pico de Gallo hot sauce (see recipe, page 164)	

1. Add beans, lime juice and garlic to the bowl of a food processor and process until smooth. Transfer to a bowl and reserve.

2. In a frying pan, heat 1 tbsp (15 mL) oil over high heat for 30 seconds. Add salt, pepper, cumin seeds and cinnamon and stir-fry for 1 minute. Add reserved bean mixture and reduce heat to medium. Stir-cook the beans for 2 to 3 minutes until the oil is absorbed and beans start to stick to the pan and are slightly scorched. Transfer to a bowl and reserve.

3. Assemble your first quesadilla: On a dry working surface, lay out one of the tortillas and spread evenly with 2 tbsp (25 mL) of the tomato sauce, then with ⅓ cup (75 mL) of the refried beans. Sprinkle 4 to 6 tbsp (60 to 90 mL) of the grated cheese over the beans, then place second tortilla on top and gently push down to stick.

4. In a large frying pan, heat 1 to 2 tbsp (15 to 25 mL) of the oil over medium high heat for 1 minute. Add quesadilla and fry for 1 to 2 minutes until crisp and slightly scorched. With a long spatula, carefully flip and fry the second side for another 1 or 2 minutes. (While it cooks, assemble your second quesadilla.)

5. When first quesadilla is ready, quickly transfer it to a cutting board. Add more oil to the pan, heat it for 30 seconds and add the next quesadilla. While it fries, cut the first one into eighths and serve immediately garnished with coriander and accompanied by Pico de Gallo sauce. Keep cooking and serving the quesadillas as soon they come off the pan.

Yam Quesadilla

SERVES UP TO 16 AS AN APPETIZER

A much simpler version of the traditional quesadilla, this one offers a meaningful contrast if served alongside its cousin, but also pleases all on its own. Composed chiefly of yam and goat cheese, it has an uncomplicated and appealing taste that is really easy to achieve. This creation courtesy of my very good friend, writer-actor Tom Rack.

Make ahead tip

Prepare yam mixture up to 2 hours ahead; keep covered and unrefrigerated.

PREHEAT OVEN TO 400°F (200°C)

1 ½ lbs	yams (about 4 small)	750 g
½ tsp	ground nutmeg	2 mL
	Salt and freshly ground black pepper to taste	
8	large (9-inch/22 cm) flour or corn tortillas	8
½ cup	finely diced red onion	125 mL
8 oz	soft goat cheese, crumbled	250 g
¼ to ½ cup	vegetable oil	50 to 125 mL
¼ cup	chopped fresh coriander	50 mL
	Salsa Cynthia (see recipe, page 165)	

1. Bake the yams whole in preheated oven for 40 to 45 minutes until easily pierced with a fork. Remove and let cool. Peel and transfer flesh to a bowl. Mash it down with a fork. Add ground nutmeg, salt and pepper and mix thoroughly.

2. Working on a dry surface, lay out one of the tortillas and spread evenly with one quarter of the yam mixture. Sprinkle with one quarter of the diced red onions, then with one quarter of the goat cheese. Top with a second tortilla and gently press down to stick.

3. In a large frying pan, heat 1 or 2 tbsp (15 or 25 mL) oil over medium high heat for 1 minute. (Use the larger quantity of oil for a crisper texture.) Fry quesadilla for 1 to 2 minutes, until crisp and slightly scorched. Carefully flip and fry the second side for another 1 or 2 minutes.

4. Repeat Steps 2 and 3 for the remaining quesadillas (while one cooks, assemble the next), adding more oil to pan for each. As soon as a quesadilla is cooked, remove from pan and cut into 8 triangles; garnish with chopped coriander and serve with Salsa Cynthia as an accompaniment. Don't wait until all the quesadillas are cooked — serve them as they come off the pan, replenishing the portions as the new ones are ready.

Soups

✤

Vegetable Stock

MAKES ABOUT 5½ CUPS (1.4 L)

No cuisine can function without its basic ingredients and stock is about as basic as ingredients get. It is the essential foundation of soups, sauces and casseroles. In my kitchen, there are two kinds of stock, which I keep on hand always. This is the more generic of the two and its uses are limitless.

✻ ✻ ✻

Tips

Stock freezes with no discernible loss. I recommend freezing it in 1-cup (250 mL) quantities for quick defrosting and access.

Double Strength: For the enhanced flavor requirements of sauces (as opposed to soups), prepare a concentrated version of this stock. Just boil down regular stock to reduce its volume by half.

Be sure to wash leeks thoroughly, splitting down the middle and paying special care to the grit that hides where the green and white parts meet.

¼ cup	olive oil	50 mL
½ tsp	fennel seeds	2 mL
2 cups	finely chopped leek, white and green parts alike (see Tips, left)	500 mL
1½ cups	finely chopped celery leaves and/or stalks, packed down	375 mL
1½ cups	finely chopped carrots	375 mL
1½ cups	finely chopped onion	375 mL
8 cups	water	2 L
2	medium parsnips, cut into chunks	2
1	bunch broccoli or head of cauliflower, stalk portion only, cut into chunks	1
2	bay leaves	2
	Several sprigs of fresh parsley and/or basil and/or coriander	
1 tsp	salt	5 mL

1. In a large saucepan or soup pot, heat olive oil over medium-high heat for 1 minute. Add fennel seeds and stir for 30 seconds. Add leek, celery, carrots and onions; cook for about 10 minutes, stirring often, until volume of ingredients is reduced by about half.

2. Add water, stirring to deglaze the pot, and mix well. Add parsnip, broccoli or cauliflower stalks, bay leaves and herb(s). Bring to boil, then reduce heat to low and let simmer undisturbed and uncovered for 30 to 35 minutes. Cover and let rest for 10 minutes.

3. Using a fine sieve, strain stock into a bowl. (Don't press down on solids; let gravity do the job.) Add salt to the stock. Store or use immediately.

Avgolemono-Rice Soup

SERVES 4

This will sound like sacrilege to my fellow Greek soup lovers, but our famous egg-lemon soup can actually be made without chicken stock and using exactly the same method. Speaking of method, I'm employing a couple of refinements (a small roux, plus the use of yolks-only instead of whole eggs) courtesy of my friend Chef Lambrino, which render the soup even more velvety and (very good news) less likely to curdle during the final heating (or during reheating).

4 cups	Vegetable Stock (see recipe, page 50)	1 L
2 tbsp	butter	25 mL
2 tbsp	all-purpose flour	25 mL
2 cups	cooked white rice	500 mL
2	egg yolks	2
3 tbsp	freshly squeezed lemon juice	45 mL
	Salt and freshly ground black pepper to taste	
	Few sprigs fresh parsley, chopped	

1. In a large saucepan, heat the vegetable stock over low heat until hot but not boiling.

2. Meanwhile, in another large saucepan or soup pot, melt butter over medium heat until bubbling (but not brown), about 1 or 2 minutes. Add flour and stir actively for 3 or 4 minutes, until all the flour is absorbed and the mixture, or roux, has returned to a bubble and is sticking slightly to the pan.

3. Add the hot stock all at once to the roux, whisking constantly, until it starts to homogenize and thicken slightly. Cook, stirring, for 2 to 3 minutes, then add the rice. Stir until well mixed, cooking for 1 minute more. Remove from heat and let rest a few minutes.

4. Meanwhile, in a large bowl, whisk together the egg yolks and lemon juice for 1 to 2 minutes. Add a small ladleful of the hot soup and beat vigorously. Continue adding small amounts and whisking until 2 cups (500 mL) of soup have been beaten into the eggs. Then add soup in a steady stream, whisking all the while, until the entire soup is emulsified.

5. Transfer soup back to the saucepan. Season soup to taste with salt and pepper. Place pan on low heat and warm the soup, stirring continuously for 4 to 5 minutes until steaming and piping hot. Remove from heat and ladle into soup bowls. Garnish with chopped parsley and serve immediately.

Avocado Soup

VEGAN RECIPE

SERVES 2

Velvety and aromatic, this soup may be eaten hot or cold — although, if served cold, you'll need to make it the night before. In either case, the fried tortilla bits are essential, and must be added to the soup directly from the frying pan. Altogether, between the fried tortillas and oil-rich avocados, this is quite a calorific affair, so it should be followed by a light main course.

✳ ✳ ✳

1	ripe avocado	1
1 tbsp	lime juice	15 mL
1	tomato	1
2 cups	Vegetable Stock (see recipe, page 50)	500 mL
2	green onions, minced	2
2 tbsp	vegetable oil	25 mL
2	small flour or corn tortillas, cut into small triangles	2
¼ cup	finely diced cucumber	50 mL
	Few sprigs fresh coriander, roughly chopped	
	Hot sauce or Salsa Cynthia (see recipe, page 165) (optional)	

1. Cut avocado in half, discard pit and spoon avocado flesh into bowl of food processor. Add lime juice.

2. Blanch tomato in boiling water for 30 seconds. Over a bowl, peel, core and deseed it. Chop tomato roughly and add to food processor. Strain any accumulated tomato juices from bowl and add to food processor.

3. In a saucepan, warm vegetable stock over low heat just until tepid. Add about half of it to food processor and blend at high speed for 30 seconds. Add the rest of the stock and blend for 1 minute more.

4. Transfer contents of food processor to a saucepan. Bring to a boil, stirring constantly, then reduce heat to minimum and simmer, stirring frequently, for about 5 minutes. Add green onions; stir and simmer for 1 minute. Turn off heat, cover and let rest 5 to 10 minutes. (If serving cold, let soup cool down and refrigerate.)

5. In a sauté or frying pan, heat vegetable oil over high heat until it's just about to smoke. Add the tortillas and fry, turning over constantly, for 1 minute or until they are golden and crispy. Remove tortilla pieces and drain on a paper towel.

6. Ladle the soup into bowls. Garnish with tortilla triangles, cucumber and coriander. If desired, add a dollop of hot sauce or salsa in the middle. Serve immediately.

Mushroom Stock

**MAKES ABOUT
6 CUPS (1.5 L)**

*With its subtle mushroom
flavor, this stock is the
heart of a clean and tasty
mushroom soup, as well as
a creamless-but-creamy
mushroom risotto
that I adore.*

※ ※ ※

Tips

This stock can also be
used to great advantage
in any sauce or other
soups that would be
enhanced by its delicate
mushroom essence.

For sauces, prepare a
concentrated version of
this stock: Just boil down
regular stock to reduce
its volume by half.

2 oz	dehydrated shiitake mushrooms	60 g
¼ cup	olive oil	50 mL
Pinch	grated nutmeg	Pinch
1½ cups	finely chopped celery leaves and/or stalks	375 mL
1½ cups	finely chopped carrots	375 mL
1½ cups	finely chopped onion	375 mL
8 cups	water	2 L
2	bay leaves	2
3	cloves	3
	Several sprigs fresh parsley and/or basil and/or coriander	
1 tsp	salt	5 mL

1. Place dehydrated shiitake mushrooms in a bowl and add sufficient boiling water to cover. Let mushrooms soak for 30 minutes, then drain (discarding liquid) and chop them into ½-inch (1 cm) pieces. Set aside.

2. In a large saucepan or soup pot, heat olive oil over medium-high heat for 1 minute. Add grated nutmeg and stir for 30 seconds. Add celery, carrots, onions and mushroom pieces. Cook, stirring often, for about 10 minutes, until volume of ingredients is reduced by about half.

3. Add water, stirring to deglaze the pot, and mix well. Add bay leaves, cloves and herb(s). Bring to boil, then reduce heat to low and let simmer undisturbed and uncovered for 30 to 35 minutes. Cover and let rest for 10 minutes.

4. Using a fine sieve, strain stock into a bowl. (Don't press down on solids; let gravity do the job.) Add salt to the stock. Store or use immediately.

Clear Mushroom Soup

SERVES 4

As delicious as it is digestible, this soup is perfect as the starter of a serious and/or festive meal. Low on fat, high on taste, it clears the palate and prepares the stomach for the onslaught to follow.

5 cups	Mushroom Stock (see recipe, page 53)	1.25 L
3 tbsp	butter	45 mL
¼ tsp	salt	1 mL
¼ tsp	freshly ground black pepper	1 mL
3 cups	sliced mushrooms (wild or regular)	750 mL
2 tbsp	freshly squeezed lemon juice	25 mL
	Several sprigs fresh parsley	

1. In a saucepan, gradually warm mushroom stock over low heat until very hot. Do not boil.

2. Meanwhile, in a large frying pan, melt butter over high heat for 1 minute until sizzling. Add salt and pepper and stir. Add sliced mushrooms and stir-fry for 5 to 6 minutes until browned. Remove from heat and stir in lemon juice.

3. Divide the mushrooms and pan juices among 4 soup bowls. Divide hot mushroom stock among bowls. Garnish with a decorative placing of 2 or 3 parsley leaves and serve immediately.

Lentil Soup Italian-Style

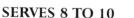

SERVES 8 TO 10

*Lentils are lovely —
plentiful, nutritious,
delicious and very adaptable.
I use them in a variety of
ways and, particularly for
winter dinner parties, this
soup is one of my favorites.
You'll find this recipe
fuss-free, since all the
ingredients are cooked
together instead of being
sautéed separately. The
double use of fennel
(both fresh and seeds),
and its natural blend with
the final cheese garnish, is
what gives this soup its
Italian credentials.*

�֎ ✖ ✖

Tips

Canned tomatoes are
most convenient, but you
can use 1½ lbs (750 g)
fresh tomatoes, blanched,
skinned and chopped.

This recipe can be easily
halved; but leftovers
freeze well and can be
reheated with minimal
loss of flavor.

2½ cups	green lentils, rinsed and drained	625 mL
12 cups	water	3 L
1 tsp	salt	5 mL
2 cups	chopped onion	500 mL
1	large carrot, diced	1
1	fennel bulb, thinly sliced (see Tip, page 142)	1
6	cloves garlic, chopped	6
1	can (28 oz/796 mL) crushed tomatoes	1
3	bay leaves	3
½ cup	chopped fresh parsley, packed down	125 mL
1½ tbsp	balsamic vinegar	20 mL
¼ cup	olive oil	50 mL
1 tsp	fennel seeds	5 mL
½ tsp	hot pepper flakes	2 mL
½ tsp	freshly ground black pepper	2 mL
	Grated Pecorino or Parmesan cheese	
	Extra virgin olive oil as accompaniment	

1. In a large saucepan or soup pot, cover lentils with the water; add salt and let lentils soak for about 20 minutes.

2. Add onions, carrots, fennel, garlic, tomatoes, bay leaves, parsley and balsamic vinegar. Bring to a boil, stirring occasionally.

3. Meanwhile, in a small frying pan, heat oil over high heat for 30 seconds. Add fennel seeds, pepper flakes and black pepper. Stir-fry for just under 1 minute and remove from heat. Set aside.

4. When the soup has come to the boil, add the oil and spices; mix well. Reduce heat to medium-low and let bubble slowly for 1 hour, stirring occasionally, until all the ingredients are soft. If the soup is too thick, add 1 to 2 cups (250 to 500 mL) water and, raising heat, bring back to a quick bubble. Take off heat, cover and let rest for 10 to 15 minutes. Serve accompanied by grated cheese and a beaker of olive oil.

French Vegetable Soup

SERVES 6 TO 8

Despite the high profile of such French soups as onion and vichyssoise, the potage of choice in France (especially on countless table d'hôte menus) is a simple purée of vegetables. Here's a fail-safe version of this standard, with a couple of enhancements of my own. I cook the soup entirely free of butter or oil — which is just as well given the fat content of the croutons and garlic mayonnaise (Aïoli) that accompany it.

Tip

Be sure to wash leeks thoroughly, splitting down the middle and paying special care to the grit that hides where the green and white parts meet.

PREHEAT OVEN TO 400°F (200°C)

1	small bunch of broccoli	1
8 cups	water	2 L
1 1/4 lbs	new potatoes, scrubbed	625 g
5 cups	leeks, green and white parts alike, roughly chopped	1.25 L
3	medium carrots, peeled	3
3	medium onions, roughly chopped	3
1 tsp	salt	5 mL
6 oz	green beans, trimmed and halved	175 g
2 cups	water	500 mL
4	thick slices of crusty bread, cut into 1-inch (2.5 cm) cubes	4
2 tbsp	olive oil	25 mL
1 tbsp	freshly squeezed lemon juice	15 mL
1/2 cup	garlic mayonnaise or Aïoli (see recipe, page 162)	125 mL
	Few sprigs fresh parsley, chopped	

1. Trim broccoli, cutting off florets and chopping the remaining stalk into three pieces. In a large saucepan or soup pot, bring water to a boil over high heat. Add broccoli stalk, potatoes, leeks, carrots, onions and salt. Bring the soup to the boil; reduce heat to medium and cook without stirring for 20 to 25 minutes, until the potatoes and carrots are softened.
2. Add broccoli florets and green beans. Cook for 15 to 20 minutes, until vegetables are tender. Remove from heat and let cool.
3. In a food processor or blender, purée the soup in batches. Transfer the purée (it will be thick) back to the soup pot, and stir in the 2 cups (500 mL) of water to achieve desired consistency. Season to taste with salt and pepper.

4. Make the croutons: Spread bread cubes in a single layer on baking sheet. Drizzle olive oil evenly over cubes. Bake in preheated oven for 8 to 10 minutes; turn croutons over and bake 5 minutes more, or until brown.

5. Reheat soup if necessary, stirring, until piping hot. Ladle the soup into wide soup plates. Sprinkle some lemon juice on each one, and garnish with the croutons. Drop a large dollop of Aïoli in the middle. Top with chopped parsley and serve immediately.

Veggie Onion Soup

SERVES 4

The French eat their signature onion soup as a meal in itself — either as a lunch with crusty baguette, or as a late-night treat, especially after a long session at the bars. This version is cooked with butter instead of the traditional lard, but comes close to the original taste nonetheless. A glass of equally traditional red wine accompanies admirably, while cutting down some of the cholesterol.

⬧ ⬧ ⬧

PREHEAT OVEN TO 450°F (230°C)
4 OVENPROOF BOWLS OR RAMEKINS, 1¹⁄₂ CUPS (375 ML) CAPACITY, MEASURING 2 INCHES (5 CM) DEEP AND ABOUT 5 INCHES (12.5 CM) WIDE

¹⁄₂ cup	butter	125 mL
¹⁄₂ tsp	freshly ground black pepper	2 mL
4 cups	thinly sliced onion	1 L
1¹⁄₂ cups	dry white wine	375 mL
4 cups	water	1 L
¹⁄₄ cup	chopped fresh parsley, packed down	50 mL
2 tbsp	soy sauce	25 mL
1 tsp	dried thyme	5 mL
2	bay leaves	2
2	cloves	2
4	large slices bread, ¹⁄₂-inch (1 cm) thick, toasted	4
3 cups	grated Swiss, mild Cheddar or Gouda cheese	750 mL

1. In a large saucepan or soup pot, melt butter over medium heat until slightly browned. Add pepper and stir. Add onions and cook, stirring, for 3 to 4 minutes, until all the onions are coated with butter. Continue cooking for another 30 minutes, stirring every 3 or 4 minutes, until the onions are creamy soft and are turning a light brown (but nowhere near burnt).

2. Add white wine and stir actively with a wooden spoon for 2 to 3 minutes, deglazing the pot and scraping up any brown bits (which give this soup its distinctive taste). Bring to a bubble and cook, stirring, for 2 to 3 minutes. Add water, parsley, soy sauce, thyme, bay leaves and cloves. Bring soup to a boil.

3. Reduce heat to medium-low, and cook for 30 minutes at a leisurely bubble, stirring occasionally. The soup is ready when reduced by about a fifth, and everything is thickly integrated. Remove from heat; cover and let rest for 1 hour to develop flavor.

4. Divide soup evenly among bowls or ramekins. Place a slice of the toasted bread to cover the surface of the soup and top each with one-quarter of the grated cheese.

5. Bake in preheated oven for 15 minutes, until the cheese is bubbling and has started to brown. Serve immediately.

Fassolada (Greek Bean Soup)

SERVES 8

The national dish of Greece, this economical, calorie-friendly, fuss-free, instantly likeable soup is chock full of flavor and nutrition. Its only drawback is that it requires hours and hours — almost days — to be ready. Normally I soak the beans overnight, and cook the soup the next day. I then refrigerate it (its flavor improves with time) and then reheat and serve it on the third day. It's worth the wait.

✳ ✳ ✳

Tips

This soup is meant to be fairly thick; if too thick, add 1 to 2 cups (250 to 500 mL) water, stir and bring back to boil.

This recipe can be easily halved; but leftovers freeze well and can be reheated with minimal loss of flavor.

2½ cups	dried white kidney beans	625 mL
1 tbsp	baking soda	15 mL
12 cups	water	3 L
1	onion, diced	1
1	large carrot, diced	1
½ cup	chopped fresh celery leaves, packed down, or 2 celery stalks, finely chopped	125 mL
2 tbsp	tomato paste	25 mL
1 tsp	freshly squeezed lemon juice	5 mL
1	medium tomato, blanched, skinned and chopped	1
1 tsp	dried rosemary, basil or oregano	5 mL
1 tsp	salt	5 mL
½ tsp	freshly ground black pepper	2 mL
¼ cup	chopped fresh parsley, packed down	50 mL
¼ cup	olive oil	50 mL
	Extra virgin olive oil, olive bits and diced red onion as garnishes	

1. In a large bowl, cover beans with plenty of warm water. Add baking soda and mix well. (The water will foam and remove some of the gas from the beans.) Let soak for at least 3 hours, preferably overnight, unrefrigerated.

2. Drain beans and transfer to a soup pot. Add plenty of water and bring to a boil. Reduce heat to medium-low and simmer for 30 minutes, occasionally skimming froth that rises to the top.

3. Drain beans; rinse and drain again. Scrub pot, cleaning off foam stuck to sides. Return beans to pot; add the 12 cups (3 L) water and place over high heat. Add onion, carrot, celery, tomato paste, lemon juice and tomato. Bring to boil, stirring; reduce heat to medium-low. Cook for 1½ hours at a rolling bubble, stirring very occasionally until beans and vegetables are very tender.

4. Add rosemary, salt, pepper, parsley and olive oil. Cook for another 5 minutes, stirring occasionally, and take off heat. Cover soup and let rest for 5 to 10 minutes. Season to taste with salt and pepper. Serve with any or all of suggested garnishes.

Salads

✦

Greek Winter Salad

SERVES 4 TO 6

There are essentially two types of Greek salad: one for the summer, when tomatoes are in season, and one for the cool months, when they are not. This may come as a surprise to many people, since Greek restaurants in North America almost invariably serve their salads with tomatoes. So here's the uncommon winter delight — the quintessential salad of the Greeks, for whom the word lettuce actually translates to salad (or "salata"). A profusion of fresh dill and green onions is what provides the special character of this dish.

1	head romaine lettuce, cut into 1/4-inch (0.5 cm) strips	1
4 or 5	green onions, green part only, cut into 1/4-inch (0.5 cm) pieces	4 or 5
	Few sprigs fresh dill, chopped	
1/4 cup	olive oil	50 mL
1 tbsp	red wine vinegar	15 mL
	Salt and freshly ground black pepper to taste	
4 oz	feta cheese, crumbled in large chunks	125 g
Pinch	dried oregano leaves	Pinch
1/2 cup	whole black olives, preferably Calamata (about 16)	125 mL

1. In a wide salad bowl, lay out lettuce strips; sprinkle with green onions and dill. Toss lightly to combine.
2. In a small bowl, whisk together olive oil and vinegar until emulsified. Season to taste with salt and pepper. Pour over the lettuce and toss well.
3. Crumble feta over the salad and sprinkle with oregano. Garnish with black olives and serve immediately.

Greek Summer Salad

SERVES 4 TO 6

Here's the salad everyone talks about. All the ingredients are widely available and can certainly be found in Greek or Middle Eastern establishments. The ripeness and flavor of the tomatoes is essential here, making this dish an expensive proposition out of season, when good tomatoes come from far away and cost a fortune.

✳ ✳ ✳

1 ½ lbs	ripe tomatoes, cut into wedges (about 6 tomatoes)	750 g
1	medium English cucumber, sliced	1
½ cup	slivered red onion	125 mL
½ cup	whole black olives (about 16)	125 mL
¼ cup	extra virgin olive oil	50 mL
2 tbsp	freshly squeezed lemon juice	25 mL
	Salt and freshly ground black pepper to taste	
4 oz	feta cheese, sliced	125 g
1 tbsp	chopped fresh oregano or 1 tsp (5 mL) dried	15 mL

1. On a large serving plate, arrange tomato wedges and cucumber slices so that they just overlap. Scatter onion slivers over everything and decorate edges of the plate with olives.

2. In a small bowl, whisk together oil, lemon juice, and salt and pepper until emulsified. Pour dressing evenly over the salad.

3. Top the salad with the feta slices (and any feta crumbles left on your cutting board). Sprinkle oregano over everything and serve within 30 minutes.

Greek Bean Salad

SERVES 6

Here is a Greek salad that hardly anyone knows. It was a popular item at my mother Despina's party buffets and tasted even better when any was left over the next day. It can be whipped up in no time, if you don't mind using canned beans.

✳ ✳ ✳

Tip

This salad can be served immediately or it can wait covered and unrefrigerated for up to 1 hour.

2 cups	cooked white kidney beans	500 mL
1	onion, thinly slivered	1
1	medium tomato, cut into ½-inch (1 cm) cubes	1
¼ cup	extra virgin olive oil	50 mL
1 tbsp	red wine vinegar	15 mL
	Salt and freshly ground black pepper to taste	
2	hard-cooked eggs, thinly sliced	2
2 cups	thinly sliced cucumber	500 mL
1 cup	drained, pickled green peppers (pepperoncini)	250 mL
¼ cup	Calamata olives (about 8)	50 mL
	Few sprigs fresh parsley, chopped	

1. Place beans in a bowl. Add slivered onion and cubed tomato. Fold gently into beans.

2. Whisk together oil and vinegar until emulsified. Add dressing to bean mixture; fold in gently but thoroughly. Season to taste with salt and pepper.

3. On a serving plate, spread out dressed beans, mounding them slightly. Decorate the borders with alternating rounds of egg and cucumber slices. Place the pickled green peppers inside this border to ring the beans. Dot the surface with the olives and garnish with chopped parsley and serve.

Avocado Soup (page 52) with Salsa Cynthia (page 165)

Overleaf (left to right): Sautéed Mushrooms on Wilted Greens (page 81), Tzatziki Sauce (page 166), Fried Zucchini (page 33) and Green and Yellow Salad (page 80)

Garlic Beets

SERVES 4 TO 6

These marinated beets live in the fridge for up to a week, providing a healthy and ever-more-flavorful side course at a moment's notice. The onion and garlic are cut thick so that they can be avoided by those on a heavy date. The old problem with beets is that they turn everything that touches them (hands, cutting board) a royal purple. Fortunately, it washes off.

1 lb	beets, unpeeled but well scrubbed	500 g
4	cloves garlic, coarsely chopped	4
1/3 cup	thickly sliced red onion	75 mL
2 tbsp	red wine vinegar	25 mL
3 tbsp	extra virgin olive oil	45 mL
	Salt and freshly ground black pepper to taste	
	Few sprigs fresh coriander and/or parsley, chopped	

1. Place beets in a large saucepan and add enough water to cover by $1\frac{1}{2}$ inches (4 cm). Bring to boil and cook beets until they can be pierced easily with a fork, about 50 to 60 minutes. If water evaporates to expose beets during cooking, replenish with more hot water.

2. Drain beets, reserving cooking liquid. Let the beets cool for about 20 minutes, then peel them (the skins should slip right off). With a sharp knife, trim the beets' tops and bottoms, as well as any small blemishes.

3. Slice beets into rounds $\frac{1}{4}$ inch (0.5 cm) thick. Transfer slices to a bowl and add garlic and onions. Sprinkle evenly with the wine vinegar and fold the mixture gently until well combined. Add olive oil and $\frac{1}{2}$ cup (125 mL) of the reserved cooking liquid. (Discard the rest of the liquid.) Mix well. Season to taste with salt and pepper and let rest for at least 20 minutes.

4. Transfer beet mixture to a serving bowl. Toss a few times. Garnish with herb(s) and serve.

Yam and Pecan Salad (page 83)

Tabbouleh

VEGAN RECIPE

SERVES 6

This may be the healthiest salad ever invented — it is certainly one of the most intriguing. Composed chiefly of parsley (normally a garnish) I'm always surprised by how much fun it is to eat (random little spikes of parsley stalk, and all). It is even a snap to make if you have one of those quick-chop machines. This recipe uses a minimum quantity of oil, because I like my tabbouleh tart. If you prefer a sweeter taste, add 2 tbsp (25 mL) more oil.

Tip

Leftover tabbouleh can be kept in the refrigerator, covered, for up to 3 days. Be sure to bring it back up to room temperature before serving.

2 cups	chopped fresh parsley, packed down	500 mL
1	medium onion, finely diced	1
1	medium tomato, finely chopped	1
1/2 cup	bulgur wheat (about 1/4 lb/125 g)	125 mL
6 tbsp	freshly squeezed lemon juice	90 mL
1/4 cup	olive oil	50 mL
	Salt and freshly ground black pepper to taste	

1. In a bowl, combine parsley, onion and tomato. Mix well. Set aside.
2. In a saucepan, boil bulgur wheat in plenty of water for 6 to 8 minutes, until tender. Drain and refresh with cold water. Drain again completely and add cooked bulgur to the vegetables in the bowl. Mix well.
3. Sprinkle lemon juice and olive oil over the salad. Add salt and pepper to taste. Toss to mix thoroughly. Transfer to a serving plate. The salad can be served immediately, although it'll be better if it waits up to 2 hours, covered and unrefrigerated.

Insalata Caprese

SERVES 4

This salad really demands tomatoes that are in season, when the aroma and sweetness of the world's most famous fruit-vegetable matches its crimson ripeness.

❈ ❈ ❈

Tip

Bocconcini are fresh, golf-ball sized mozzarella curds that must be kept in water until they are needed. They are widely available. In supermarkets, they usually sit in plastic tubs right by the ricotta and other Italian dairy products.

1 lb	ripe tomatoes, sliced ½ inch (1 cm) thick (about 4 tomatoes)	500 g
¼ cup	thinly sliced red onion	50 mL
¼ cup	thinly sliced green bell peppers	50 mL
¼ cup	extra virgin olive oil	50 mL
2 tbsp	balsamic vinegar	25 mL
	Salt and freshly ground black pepper to taste	
6 oz	bocconcini (see Tip, left)	175 g
¼ cup	Calamata olives (about 8)	50 mL
12	large leaves fresh basil	12

1. On a large presentation plate, arrange tomato slices in one layer. Scatter sliced onions and green peppers evenly over the tomatoes.

2. In a small bowl, whisk together oil, vinegar, salt and pepper until emulsified. Pour dressing evenly over the tomatoes.

3. Drain and pat dry the bocconcini. Slice into rounds ¼ inch (0.5 cm) thick. Put at least one slice of cheese on top of each tomato slice.

4. Place olives decoratively among the tomatoes. Garnish with the basil leaves, and serve within 30 minutes.

Roasted Peppers Antipasto

SERVES 4

The flesh of a bell pepper bathed in olive oil offers a taste and texture sensation like no other. It has only one drawback: the dreary chore of roasting or grilling the pepper, then trying to peel, core and deseed the blackened vegetable with its messy wet innards.

✳ ✳ ✳

Tips

To save time and trouble, I core and cut my peppers in half before roasting or grilling. This tends to dehydrate and shrink the flesh a little, making it fragile, but it's a heck of a lot easier.

For parties, try serving these peppers with black olives, sun-dried tomatoes, capers, sliced ripe tomatoes, mozzarella or bocconcini cheese, artichoke hearts and marinated mushrooms to create a real Italian appetizer extravaganza.

The antipasto can be made ahead and kept, covered and refrigerated, for up to 2 days.

PREHEAT OVEN TO 400°F (200°C)

3	bell peppers, preferably different colors (eg. green, red and yellow)	3
1 tsp	vegetable oil	5 mL
1 tbsp	balsamic vinegar	15 mL
¼ cup	extra virgin olive oil	50 mL
	Salt and freshly ground black pepper to taste	
2 oz	Parmesan cheese, shaved	60 g
¼ cup	thinly sliced red onion	50 mL
	Few sprigs of fresh basil and/or parsley, chopped	

1. Cut peppers in half lengthwise, then core and deseed them. Brush their skins with the vegetable oil, and arrange the peppers (without crowding) in an oven pan, skin side up. Roast in preheated oven for 20 to 25 minutes, just until the skin has crinkled but before it has blackened. (If you wait until the skin turns black, the flesh of these halved peppers will totally disintegrate.) Remove peppers from oven and let cool 5 to 10 minutes.

2. Using a spatula, pry the cooled peppers from the pan and transfer them to a work surface. Remove the skins — they should come off easily and more or less in one piece. Cut each into 5 or 6 strips and transfer to a plate.

3. Moisten the pepper strips with balsamic vinegar, then douse them with the olive oil. Add salt and pepper to taste. Decorate with the Parmesan shavings, onions and basil and/or parsley just prior to serving. The oiled peppers will wait (and improve) for up to 1 hour.

Marinated Mushrooms

SERVES 4 TO 6

This is a refreshing and meaningful appetizer or side vegetable that requires next to no cooking. It can sit nicely in the fridge for up to 2 days while waiting to be needed, improving its flavor all the while.

5 cups	mushrooms, washed and trimmed	1.25 L
1/4 cup	slivered red onion	50 mL
3	cloves garlic, minced	3
1/4 cup	walnut pieces	50 mL
1 tsp	olive oil	5 mL
6 tbsp	extra virgin olive oil	90 mL
2 tbsp	white wine vinegar	25 mL
1 tbsp	soy sauce	15 mL
Pinch	cayenne pepper (optional)	Pinch
	Salt and freshly ground black pepper to taste	
	Few sprigs fresh parsley and/or basil, chopped	

1. In a bowl, toss mushrooms, red onions and garlic until well mixed.

2. In a small frying pan over medium heat, stir-fry walnut pieces in 1 tsp (5 mL) olive oil for 1 to 2 minutes, being careful not to let them burn. Add to mushroom mixture.

3. In a small bowl, whisk together 6 tbsp (90 mL) olive oil, vinegar, soy sauce, salt, pepper and cayenne, if using, until emulsified. Add dressing to salad and fold gently until the vegetables are well coated. Season to taste with salt and pepper. Leave uncovered for at least 1 hour, gently folding every 15 minutes or so. Transfer to a serving bowl, and garnish liberally with the herb(s). Serve immediately or keep for up to 1 hour more, covered and unrefrigerated.

Portobello Mushrooms with Goat Cheese

SERVES 2

Exotic-sounding name notwithstanding, portobello mushrooms are nothing more than overgrown regular mushrooms. But for some alchemical reason their taste is very different (more meaty) from those lowly buttons. As a result they are usually associated with "wild" (or "fancy") mushrooms and are very much in demand. Luckily, they are available everywhere and often, quite conveniently, already trimmed and sliced into attractive ¹/₂-inch (1 cm) slices.

✻ ✻ ✻

Tip

Green peppercorns are sold packed in brine; leftovers will keep if refrigerated in their original brine. While optional, they are delicious in this recipe.

PREHEAT BROILER
BAKING SHEET

2 tbsp	olive oil	25 mL
6 oz	portobello mushrooms, trimmed and sliced ¹/₂ inch (1 cm) thick	175 g
1 tbsp	finely chopped garlic	15 mL
2 tsp	balsamic vinegar, divided	10 mL
¹/₄ tsp	salt	1 mL
¹/₈ tsp	freshly ground black pepper	0.5 mL
¹/₄ tsp	drained green peppercorns (optional)	1 mL
2 oz	goat cheese	60 g
2 tsp	pine nuts	10 mL
	Several lettuce leaves	
2 tsp	olive oil	10 mL

1. In a nonstick frying pan, heat 2 tbsp (25 mL) olive oil over high heat for 1 minute. Add mushroom slices in one layer; cook 2 to 3 minutes or until nicely browned (they will absorb all the oil). Turn and cook second side for under a minute. Add garlic, 1 tsp (5 mL) of the balsamic vinegar, salt and pepper; continue cooking for 1 minute to brown the garlic somewhat.

2. Remove from heat. Arrange on baking sheet in 2 flat piles about 3 inches (7.5 cm) wide. Sprinkle evenly with green peppercorns, if using. Divide the goat cheese in two; make each half into a thick disk, about 1 inch (2.5 cm) wide. Place a disk of cheese on each pile of mushrooms. Sprinkle the pine nuts evenly over the piles, some on the cheese and some on the surrounding mushrooms. (The recipe can wait at this point up to 1 hour, covered and unrefrigerated.)

3. Broil the mushrooms for just under 4 minutes or until the cheese is soft and a little brown, and the pine nuts are dark brown.

4. Line 2 plates with lettuce. Carefully lift each pile off the baking sheet and transfer as intact as possible onto the lettuce. Sprinkle about 1 tsp (5 mL) olive oil and $\frac{1}{2}$ tsp (2 mL) balsamic vinegar over each portion and serve immediately.

Sautéed Eggplant Salad

SERVES 4

An oily pleasure, eggplant is such a joy to eat that we tend to forgive it all its excesses. A huge favorite in southern Europe (and all over the sunbelt), it appears in countless recipes. Our adaptation appears here, using ratatouille as a base and touching on the various stewed and sautéed eggplant salads of the Middle East.

❋ ❋ ❋

Tip

The chilies were an enhancement to please the "heat" requirements of the cast and crew of *Love! Valour! Compassion!*, whose filming we catered. If you like things less spicy, just omit the chili flakes.

4 cups	eggplant, cut into ½-inch (1 cm) cubes	1 L
	Salted water	
3 tbsp	vegetable oil	45 mL
3 tbsp	olive oil	45 mL
½ tsp	salt	2 mL
¼ tsp	freshly ground black pepper	1 mL
¼ tsp	hot pepper flakes	1 mL
1	onion, cut into ¼-inch (0.5 cm) slices	1
½	green bell pepper, cut into ½-inch (1 cm) squares	½
½	red bell pepper, cut into ½-inch (1 cm) squares	½
4	cloves garlic, thinly sliced	4
4	sun-dried tomatoes, thinly sliced	4
1	medium tomato, cut into ½-inch (1 cm) wedges	1
1 tsp	red wine vinegar	5 mL
½ tsp	dried basil leaves	2 mL
½ tsp	dried oregano leaves	2 mL
¼ cup	water	50 mL
	Few sprigs chopped fresh basil and/or parsley	

1. Immerse cubed eggplant in cold salted water as soon as possible after cutting it (eggplant turns brown soon after it is cut); let soak 5 to 10 minutes.

2. In a large nonstick frying pan, heat vegetable oil over medium-high heat for 1 minute. Drain eggplant and add to the pan (watch for splutters). It will absorb all the oil almost immediately. Cook, stirring actively, for 6 to 7 minutes or until the eggplant is soft and browned all over. Transfer the cooked eggplant to a dish; set aside.

3. Using the same frying pan, heat olive oil over medium-high heat for 30 seconds. Add salt, pepper and hot pepper flakes; stir-fry for 30 seconds. Add onion, green and red pepper; stir-fry 2 to 3 minutes or until wilted and beginning to char. Add garlic and sun-dried tomatoes; stir-fry 1 minute. Add tomato, vinegar, basil and oregano; stir-fry 2 minutes or until tomato has broken down and a sauce is forming. Add water and immediately reduce heat to medium. Stir in eggplant. Gently mix and fold all ingredients together; cook 2 minutes or until heated through.

4. Transfer to a flat dish and let rest for about 10 minutes. Garnish with fresh herbs. Serve lukewarm.

Eggplant with Mint

VEGAN RECIPE

SERVES 4

All Mediterranean cultures roast or grill their eggplant, transforming an otherwise spongy vegetable into a creamy vessel for olive oil and garlic. Babaganoush and Greek eggplant purée (without tahini) are labor-intensive preparations that are more akin to dips than salads. This Sicilian recipe is just as tasty; but since you don't mash the eggplant, it requires a lot less elbow grease

Tip

When working with hot peppers, be sure to wear gloves; otherwise, wash hands thoroughly.

PREHEAT OVEN TO 450°F (230°C)

1	large eggplant (about 1 1/2 lbs/750 g)	1
1 tsp	vegetable oil	5 mL
1/4 cup	olive oil	50 mL
2 tbsp	freshly squeezed lemon juice	25 mL
2 tbsp	chopped fresh mint or 1 tbsp (15 mL) dried	25 mL
3	cloves garlic, minced	3
1	fresh chili, finely chopped (with or without seeds, depending on desired hotness)	1
	Salt to taste	
1	small tomato, cut into wedges	1
1/4 cup	black olives (about 8)	50 mL

1. Brush eggplant lightly with vegetable oil. Using a fork, pierce the skin lightly at 1-inch (2.5 cm) intervals. Place on an oven pan and bake for 1 hour.
2. Meanwhile prepare the dressing: In a small bowl combine the olive oil, lemon juice, mint, garlic and chili (with seeds, if desired); mix well and set aside.
3. Transfer eggplant to a work surface. Cut off 1 inch (2.5 cm) at the stem end and discard (this part never quite cooks through). Peel the eggplant by picking at an edge from the cut end, then pulling upward. The skin should come off easily in strips.
4. Cut the eggplant lengthwise and place each half with the interior facing you. With a spoon scoop out the tongues of seed-pods, leaving as much of the flesh as possible. To remove the additional seed-pods hiding inside, cut each piece of eggplant in half and repeat the deseeding procedure. Once deseeded, cut the eggplant flesh into strips 2 inches (5 cm) long and 1 inch (2.5 cm) wide. Transfer the strips to a serving bowl.
5. Whisk the reserved dressing and add salt to taste. Add to the eggplant. Fold gently to dress all the pieces, then garnish with tomato wedges and black olives. Serve right away, or let wait covered and unrefrigerated for up to 2 hours.

French Potato Salad

VEGAN RECIPE

SERVES 8

Here's a version of the old picnic standard that uses no mayonnaise and will therefore keep better on a warm day. It is also wonderful to eat freshly made, while still lukewarm.

2 lbs	new potatoes, unpeeled but well scrubbed	1 kg
1/4 cup	dry white wine	50 mL
3 tbsp	French whole-grain mustard	45 mL
2 tbsp	white wine vinegar	25 mL
1	medium red onion, slivered	1
	Few sprigs fresh parsley, chopped	
1/4 cup	olive oil	50 mL
	Salt and freshly ground black pepper to taste	
1/4 cup	whole black olives (about 8)	50 mL

1. Boil potatoes over high heat for 10 to 15 minutes, or until easily pierced with a fork, but not yet crumbling. Drain and transfer to a cutting board. Slice the hot potatoes (using a cloth to handle them) into 1/4-inch (0.5 cm) rounds. Transfer slices to a bowl.
2. In a small bowl, whisk together wine, mustard and vinegar until emulsified. Drizzle over the potato slices and toss gently until well coated.
3. Scatter red onion and parsley over the potatoes, then drizzle with olive oil. Toss gently until well combined. Season to taste with salt and pepper.
4. Transfer salad to a serving bowl and garnish with black olives. Serve immediately or keep for up to 4 hours, covered and unrefrigerated, until ready to serve.

Avocado Salad

SERVES 2

No other fruit, not even the tomato, can supplant the glorious avocado as the centerpiece of an appetizer salad. The avocado's subtle and refreshing taste can be enhanced in a variety of ways and its oil content (considerable, to say the least) satisfies any hunger pangs that arise while awaiting the main course. In this book I offer three salad recipes for this magic ingredient, starting with this uncomplicated, colorful salad.

1 tbsp	lime juice	15 mL
1	ripe avocado	1
¼ cup	slivered red bell peppers	50 mL
¼ cup	slivered red onion	50 mL
2 tbsp	vegetable oil	25 mL
	Salt and freshly ground black pepper to taste	
	Few sprigs fresh coriander, chopped	
	Salsa Cynthia (see recipe, page 165) or Pico de Gallo (see recipe, page 164)	
	Corn chips	

1. Put lime juice in a small bowl. Peel avocado and cut into slices (or scoop out with a small spoon) and add to the lime juice. Toss gently until well coated. Add red peppers and onions; drizzle with oil. Toss gently until all ingredients are thoroughly combined. Season to taste with salt and pepper.

2. Transfer salad to a serving plate and spread out attractively. Garnish with chopped coriander and serve within 1 hour, accompanied by hot sauce and corn chips.

Avocado Melissa Sue Anderson

VEGAN RECIPE

SERVES 8 TO 10

Best remembered for her role in television's Little House on the Prairie, *the young actress after whom this salad is named later starred in the bizarre (and gory) horror film,* Happy Birthday to Me. *It was on the set of this cinematic masterpiece that I, in my role as caterer, created this colorful, West-Coast-style concoction. Ms. Anderson loved it so much that she had it every day for lunch over the entire seven weeks of shooting. This is one of those salads you put together during a sunny day on the patio, slicing lovely things into a large bowl, adding layer upon layer of color, as the sound of the distant surf dissolves into friendly conversation. At the end, you toss it all together gently, and offer it to your assembled friends. In fact, it's such a good party dish that I offer a large recipe for buffet-style service to a number of guests.*

2 tbsp	lime juice	25 mL
2	ripe avocados	2
1	Granny Smith apple, peeled and thinly sliced	1
2	peaches, peeled and cut into chunks	2
5	green onions, cut into 1/2-inch (1 cm) pieces	5
3 cups	sliced mushrooms	750 mL
2	sticks celery, chopped	2
3/4 cup	unpeeled, diced English cucumber	175 mL
2	tomatoes, cubed	2
1/3 cup	toasted cashew pieces	75 mL
3 tbsp	finely chopped fresh coriander	45 mL
2 tbsp	vegetable oil	25 mL
1 tbsp	sesame oil	15 mL
1 tbsp	raspberry or white wine vinegar	15 mL
1 tsp	salt	5 mL
1 tsp	cayenne pepper (optional)	5 mL
	Alfalfa sprouts	

1. Put lime juice in a large bowl. Peel avocado and cut into slices (or scoop out with a small spoon) and add to the lime juice. Toss gently until well coated. Add apple slices and toss again. Add peaches, green onions, mushrooms, celery, cucumber, tomato and cashew pieces.
2. In a small bowl, whisk together coriander, vegetable oil, sesame oil, vinegar, salt and cayenne, if using, until emulsified. Drizzle half of the dressing over the salad. Fold in the dressing, mixing the various ingredients of the salad. Do this gently but thoroughly. Add the rest of the dressing, and fold in 5 or 6 more times.
3. Transfer to a serving bowl and garnish with alfalfa sprouts for that final California touch. Serve immediately or keep up to 1 hour, covered and unrefrigerated.

Lentil and Beet Salad

SERVES 4 TO 6

*Writer-producer,
ex(traordinary) neighbor,
and all-around fabulous
person, Sharon Corder,
created this earthy/swarthy
salad for the dinner parties
she and hubby Jack Blum
seem to throw at will.
It's surprisingly light,
considering its weighty
ingredients, and easy to
make — save for the time
it takes to boil those pesky
beets (and cleaning up
the blood-red stains that
inevitably result).*

✻ ✻ ✻

Tip

If possible, prepare your
own lentils instead of
using the canned variety.
Use 1 cup (250 mL) dry
lentils boiled in salted
water for 20 minutes
to get 2 cups (500 mL)
cooked, drained lentils.

1 lb	beets, unpeeled but well scrubbed	500 g
2 cups	cooked green lentils (see Tip, left)	500 mL
1/2 cup	finely diced red bell peppers	125 mL
1/4 cup	finely diced red onion	50 mL
1	stick celery, finely diced	1
1 tbsp	grated lemon zest	15 mL
1 tbsp	walnut oil	15 mL
1/2 tsp	ground cumin	2 mL
1/2 cup	chopped walnuts	125 mL
3 tbsp	freshly squeezed lemon juice	45 mL
1 1/2 tbsp	red wine vinegar	20 mL
3	cloves garlic, minced	3
Pinch	ground nutmeg	Pinch
3 tbsp	walnut oil	45 mL
	Salt and freshly ground black pepper to taste	
1	bunch beet greens	1
	Few sprigs fresh dill, chopped	

1. Place beets in a large saucepan and add enough water to cover by 1 1/2 inches (4 cm). Bring to boil and cook beets until they can be pierced easily with a fork, about 50 to 60 minutes. If water evaporates to expose beets during cooking, replenish with more hot water. Drain the liquid and allow the beets to cool; peel, trim, and cut into 1/4-inch (0.5 cm) cubes.

2. Transfer the beets to a bowl. Add lentils, red peppers, red onions, celery and lemon zest. Mix thoroughly. The salad will have turned a dark red.

3. In a small frying pan, heat 1 tbsp (15 mL) walnut oil over medium-high heat for 30 seconds. Add ground cumin and stir for 30 seconds. Add chopped walnuts and stir-fry for 2 minutes, until starting to brown. Add to the salad, scraping off the cumin and oil from the pan; toss gently.

4. In a small bowl, whisk together lemon juice, vinegar, garlic and nutmeg; add 3 tbsp (45 mL) walnut oil, whisking to emulsify. Pour over the salad and fold everything together. Season to taste with salt and pepper.

5. Steam or boil the beet greens for no more than 2 minutes; drain immediately and refresh in iced water. Trim the stalks and discard. Arrange the leaves around the rim of a serving plate.

6. Transfer salad to the center of the plate and garnish liberally with chopped dill. This salad can be served immediately or it can wait for up to 2 hours, covered and unrefrigerated.

Green and Yellow Salad

SERVES 4 TO 6

Parrot green and mellow yellow, this refreshing concoction successfully combines the al dente crunch of fresh beans, with the rich smoothness of ripe avocado. The perky dressing, which features the unusual partnering of feta cheese with lime/coriander (instead of the more obvious lemon/oregano), serves to unify the various flavors. The salad works just as well with only green (instead of green and yellow) beans, although at the cost of its visual appeal.

✷ ✷ ✷

8 oz	fresh green beans, trimmed	250 g
8 oz	fresh yellow beans, trimmed	250 g
1 tbsp	lime juice	15 mL
1	ripe avocado	1
	Salt and freshly ground black pepper to taste	
3 tbsp	olive oil	45 mL
3	green onions, finely chopped	3
4 oz	feta cheese, crumbled into large chunks	125 g
	Few sprigs fresh coriander, roughly chopped	

1. Boil green and yellow beans over high heat for 5 to 7 minutes. Drain and immediately refresh in a bowl of ice-cold water. Drain, and put in a wide salad bowl.

2. Put lime juice in a bowl. Peel avocado and cut into slices (or scoop out with a small spoon), and add to the lime juice. Fold avocado into the juice until well coated. Scatter avocado slices (or scoops) decoratively over the beans, along with any leftover lime juice. Season to taste with salt and pepper.

3. Drizzle olive oil over salad, and garnish with chopped green onions. Distribute feta over the salad, and top with a scattering of the chopped coriander. The salad can wait up to 1 hour, covered and unrefrigerated.

Sautéed Mushrooms on Wilted Greens

SERVES 8

This concoction of garlicky, succulent mushrooms served over your preferred greens makes a simple but deluxe first course for important dinners. It's fast, it's yummy, and it will quickly become your favorite — as it is mine. The crucial element of this dish is the quality of the mushrooms. Ordinary mushrooms will work in a pinch, but the luxurious texture and flavor of oyster or portobello mushrooms justifies the extra cost. This recipe can be easily halved for smaller gatherings.

※ ※ ※

Variation

If desired, use 1 lb (500 g) whole oyster mushrooms, trimmed, instead of the portobello mushroom strips.

1 lb	lettuce (one type or mixture of several types), washed, dried and torn into bite-size pieces	500 g
6 tbsp	olive oil	90 mL
1/2 tsp	salt	2 mL
1/2 tsp	freshly ground black pepper	2 mL
3/4 cup	thinly sliced red onion	175 mL
4 cups	thickly sliced portobello mushrooms	1 L
6	cloves garlic, finely chopped	6
2 tbsp	freshly squeezed lemon juice	25 mL
2 tbsp	white wine	25 mL
1	medium tomato, cut into wedges	1
1/4	red bell pepper, cut into thin half-rounds	1/4
1 tbsp	grated lemon zest	15 mL
	Few sprigs fresh parsley, roughly chopped	

1. Place lettuce in a large salad bowl.

2. In a large frying pan, heat olive oil over high heat. Add salt and pepper and stir. Add sliced red onions and stir-fry for 1 minute. Add mushrooms and stir-fry actively, for 4 to 5 minutes, until they are shiny and beginning to char slightly. Add garlic and stir-fry for 1 minute. Add lemon juice and let come to a sizzle, about 30 seconds. Add wine and stir-fry for 1 to 2 minutes, until a syrupy sauce has formed.

3. Transfer the contents of the frying pan with all its juices, evenly over the lettuce. Use a fork to arrange the mushrooms decoratively. Garnish with tomato wedges, red pepper crescents and lemon zest. Top with some chopped parsley, and serve immediately. Toss gently at table, leaving most of the mushrooms on top.

Mango-Cucumber Salad

SERVES 4 TO 6

This sweet-and-sour salad is extremely versatile, and was inspired by my association with Wandee Young and the Thai cookbook I wrote with her. It combines the fundamental elements of two of Thailand's most delicious side dishes into a brand new concoction that can accompany a wide array of main courses. It also keeps well in the fridge and leftovers can be served the next day.

✻ ✻ ✻

Tip

Here's the Thai way to create the julienne strips of mango: hold the mango firmly in your hand and with a sharp knife, make a number of closely spaced parallel cuts into surface facing you, then slice thinly to get shreds. Turn over and repeat procedure with the other half. Be warned, though: this technique can lead to bloodshed if there is a slip-up.

1	8-inch (20 cm) section of unpeeled English cucumber cut lengthwise into quarters, then thinly sliced	1
1	green mango, peeled and cut into julienne strips (see Tip, left)	1
¼ cup	slivered red onion	50 mL
3	green onions, finely chopped	3
2 tbsp	finely chopped fresh coriander	25 mL
½	red bell pepper, cut into thin strips	½
1	jalapeño pepper, finely chopped (with or without seeds, depending on desired hotness)	1
2 tbsp	lime juice	25 mL
2 tbsp	white vinegar	25 mL
2 tbsp	vegetable oil	25 mL
1 tbsp	granulated sugar	15 mL
	Salt to taste	

1. Put cucumber and mango into a large bowl. Add the red onions, green onions, half of the coriander (reserving the rest), red pepper and jalapeño. Toss until well mixed.

2. In a small bowl, whisk together lime juice, vinegar, oil and sugar until emulsified. Season to taste with salt. Pour dressing over salad, and toss well. Transfer to a serving bowl and garnish with the remainder of the chopped coriander. Serve immediately or keep for up to 2 hours, covered and unrefrigerated.

Yam and Pecan Salad

VEGAN RECIPE

SERVES 4 TO 6

This is a spectacular salad that will gain new fans for the sweet smoothness of the nutritious but neglected yam. The pecans are a slight extravagance (both financial and caloric), but they add crunch and significant luxury. The colorful concoction works as a lively appetizer, as well as one course of a celebratory, slightly exotic buffet.

PREHEAT OVEN TO 450°F (230°C)
BAKING DISH, GREASED WITH 1 TBSP (15 mL) VEGETABLE OIL

1 lb	yams, unpeeled but well scrubbed	500 g
½	red bell pepper, cut into thick strips	½
¼ cup	vegetable oil	50 mL
1 tsp	mustard seeds	5 mL
Pinch	cayenne pepper	Pinch
Pinch	ground cinnamon	Pinch
Pinch	ground cumin	Pinch
⅓ cup	pecan halves	75 mL
3 tbsp	lime juice	45 mL
1 tsp	sesame oil	5 mL
½ tsp	salt	2 mL
½ cup	thinly slivered red onion	125 mL
	Few sprigs fresh coriander, chopped	

1. In a large saucepan, cover yams with plenty of water and bring to a boil. Cook for 10 minutes, then drain. Cut yams into rounds ½ inch (1 cm) thick.

2. In prepared baking dish, arrange the sliced yams and red pepper strips in a single layer. Bake in preheated oven for 12 to 15 minutes, until the yams are easily pierced with a fork.

3. Meanwhile, in a frying pan, heat oil over medium heat for 1 minute. Add mustard seeds, cayenne, cinnamon and cumin, and stir-fry for 2 minutes, or until spices begin to pop. Add the pecans; stir-fry for 2 minutes until the nuts have browned a little on both sides (don't burn them). Remove from heat and reserve spices in pan.

4. Remove yams and red peppers from the oven. Using a spatula, carefully transfer them onto a serving plate, making a single layer.

5. Drizzle lime juice and sesame oil over the yams and sprinkle with salt. Scatter slivers of red onion on top. Using a spoon and a rubber spatula, scrape contents of the frying pan (pecans, oil and spices) evenly over the yams. Let salad rest for 10 to 15 minutes, then garnish with the chopped coriander and serve.

Don Don Noodles

SERVES 4 TO 6

This cold noodle specialty is one of the inexpensive street foods of China's Szechwan province. It's sweet and spicy and hits the spot perfectly as the curtain-raiser to a high-voltage meal. Do not serve these if the rest of the meal has subtle tastes.

❋ ❋ ❋

Tip

The sesame sauce used here is sold bottled in Chinese markets. The oil tends to separate from the solids, which are hard and dense. So when using it for this recipe, try to scoop out some of the oil along with the solids. The rest will keep well and can be used instead of tahini in other recipes. (Tahini is unsuitable for this sauce: it's too sweet and not nutty enough.)

8 oz	dry Chinese noodles (wheat, not rice)	250 g
1 tbsp	sesame oil	15 mL
3 tbsp	Chinese sesame sauce (see Tip, left)	45 mL
½ cup	warm water	125 mL
2	cloves garlic, minced	2
1 tbsp	minced gingerroot	15 mL
1 tbsp	soy sauce or tamari sauce	15 mL
1 tsp	granulated sugar	5 mL
½ tsp	freshly ground black pepper	2 mL
3	green onions, finely chopped	3
½ cup	finely diced cucumber	125 mL
	Asian Hot Oil (see recipe, page 160)	

1. In a pot of boiling water, cook noodles until they are al dente. Drain and refresh with cold water several times. Transfer to a bowl and sprinkle with sesame oil; toss well. Cover and refrigerate for to 2 or 3 hours.

2. Make the sauce: Spoon sesame sauce into a bowl. Mash it with a fork to loosen it, and whisk in warm water a little at a time. The lumps will disappear after 2 to 3 minutes of whisking. Add garlic, ginger, soy, sugar and black pepper; whisk until very smooth. The sauce can now wait, covered and unrefrigerated, for up to several hours.

3. When ready to serve, divide cold noodles between 4 to 6 bowls. Top each with equal spoonfuls of the sauce. Do not mix in: that happens at table. Garnish with the green onions and cucumber. Serve immediately, accompanied by a bowl of hot oil, drops of which are added at table to taste.

Istanbul Leeks

SERVES 4

This was one of my mother Despina's favorite "everyday" recipes. Perfect for a light lunch on its own, this savory dish works equally well as an accompaniment to meat or chicken for dinner. Istanbul gourmets eat these leeks (or prassa) at room temperature — as they do all their oil-cooked (versus butter-cooked) vegetables. Also, my mother, being an old-style Mediterranean, used at least twice as much oil as I (a more modern Med gourmet) suggest in this recipe. Vegetable oil is better than olive oil here, since it has a lighter taste. And, as always with leeks, care must be taken to wash out the grit that hides inside this flavorful vegetable.

1 lb	leeks (about 4 medium)	500 g
1/4 cup	vegetable oil	50 mL
1 tsp	sweet paprika	5 mL
1 tsp	salt	5 mL
1/2 tsp	freshly ground black pepper	2 mL
1/2 cup	short-grain rice	125 mL
2	carrots, scraped and cut into 1/4-inch (0.5 cm) rounds	2
2 cups	boiling water	500 mL
1 tsp	granulated sugar	5 mL
2 tbsp	freshly squeezed lemon juice	25 mL

1. To ensure that the leeks do not separate, make a 3-inch (7.5 cm) slit lengthwise through the middle of each leek. Wash sand away from central layers (where the white and green meet) through this slit. Cut off fibrous stem and discard. Slice the rest of the leek (green and white parts alike) into 1/2-inch (1 cm) chunks. Set aside.

2. In a pot, heat oil with paprika, salt and pepper for 1 minute over medium-high heat, stirring. Add rice; stir-fry 2 minutes or until oily and sizzling. Add leeks and carrots; stir-fry 2 minutes or until everything is shiny and beginning to fry. Add water and sugar; stir to settle the ingredients, reduce heat to low and cover the pot tightly. Let cook for 35 to 40 minutes or until the vegetables and rice are tender and much of the moisture has been absorbed.

3. Remove from heat and let stand alone, covered, for about 10 minutes. Uncover, sprinkle with lemon juice and stir gently. Serve immediately or let cool and serve at room temperature.

Summer Artichoke Salad

SERVES 4

Baby artichokes are a gift of nature. Here we find all the glory of grown-up artichokes, but with an edible choke (the fuzz that grows out and protects the heart) — which means zero work and all pleasure.

Even more to the point, baby artichokes come to us already cooked (well, a bit overcooked) and ready to use. They're available bottled in oil or canned in water. If using ready-made, I recommend the canned. If using fresh, remove the outer leaves, cut 1/2 inch (1 cm) off the top, trim the stalk and boil over medium heat for 15 minutes until the hearts (bottoms) are easily pierced.

✳ ✳ ✳

6	baby artichokes, cooked or 14-oz (398 mL) can artichoke hearts, rinsed and drained	6
1/2	red bell pepper, cut into thin strips	1/2
1/4 cup	thinly sliced red onion	50 mL
1	1-inch (2.5 cm) piece English cucumber, thinly sliced	1
5	black olives, pitted and halved	5
1	ripe large tomato, cut into 1/2-inch (1 cm) wedges	1
12	seedless grapes, halved	12
1 tsp	drained capers	5 mL
1	clove garlic, pressed	1
2 tbsp	extra virgin olive oil	25 mL
1 tbsp	white wine vinegar	15 mL
1 tbsp	freshly squeezed lemon juice	15 mL
1/4 tsp	salt	1 mL
1/8 tsp	freshly ground black pepper	0.5 mL
	Few sprigs fresh parsley, chopped	

1. Cut artichokes in half and put in a salad bowl. Add red pepper, onions, cucumber, olives, tomato, grapes and capers. Toss gently to mix.

2. In a small bowl, whisk together garlic, olive oil, vinegar, lemon juice, salt and pepper until slightly emulsified. Drizzle over the salad and toss gently to dress all the pieces, but without breaking up the artichokes too much. Garnish with parsley, and serve within 1 hour (cover if it has to wait, but do not refrigerate).

Daniaile's "Little" Cauliflower Salad

SERVES 6

Cauliflower is a beautiful vegetable, although a puzzling one. Not quite tasty enough raw, it inevitably overcooks and tastes "off" if its florets are boiled whole. My great friend Daniaile Jarry found that if chopped into match-head-size bits and boiled quickly, cauliflower retains both flavor and texture. Here's a salad — dubbed "le petit choux-fleur de Daniaile" — that mixes these cauliflower bits with potatoes and aromatics.

1	head cauliflower	1
1 lb	potatoes, peeled and cut into ½-inch (1 cm) cubes (about 3 cups/750 mL)	500 g
1 cup	thinly sliced red onion	250 mL
½	green pepper, very finely diced	½
2 tbsp	drained capers	25 mL
2 tbsp	white wine vinegar	25 mL
1 tbsp	Dijon mustard	15 mL
1 tsp	salt	5 mL
½ tsp	freshly ground black pepper	2 mL
⅓ cup	extra virgin olive oil	75 mL
	Several sprigs fresh parsley, chopped	

1. Separate florets of cauliflower from the large stalks. Reserve stalks for another use. Chop florets into tiny bits (match-head size). You should get about 4 cups (1 L). Set aside.

2. Boil potatoes in salted water on high heat for 5 to 6 minutes or until tender. Add reserved cauliflower bits and wait until water resumes boiling; from this point, boil for another 2 minutes or until the cauliflower is starting to become tender but is still crunchy. Drain immediately. Do not run cold water over the drained vegetables.

3. Transfer potatoes and cauliflower into a working bowl while still piping hot. Add onions, green pepper and capers. Toss gently a couple of times to mix.

4. In a small bowl, combine vinegar, mustard, salt and pepper. Add olive oil and whisk to combine. Pour sauce evenly over the vegetables. Toss gently but thoroughly to mix all the ingredients with the dressing.

5. If serving immediately (while still warm), transfer to a dish and garnish liberally with parsley. If for a buffet, the salad can wait up to 2 hours, covered and unrefrigerated. When ready to serve, mix to redistribute the dressing, transfer to a dish and garnish with parsley.

Moroccan Grapefruit and Olive Salad

SERVES 4

Here's a dish that does great service as a light opening course and admirably on the side of things like couscous, paella or lasagna. The success of this delicious, very "adult" salad depends on its appearance which, in turn, depends on whether you're able to peel and skin the grapefruit segments while keeping them intact. Oranges can substitute for grapefruit — although they're even more tedious to prepare. Using ready-skinned segments is always an option.

2	grapefruits	2
1/2 cup	thinly sliced red onion	125 mL
8	black olives, pitted and chopped in slivers	8
3 tbsp	extra virgin olive oil	45 mL
1 tbsp	white wine vinegar	15 mL
1 tsp	freshly squeezed lemon juice	5 mL
1/2 tsp	sweet paprika	2 mL
1/2 tsp	salt	2 mL
1/4 tsp	freshly ground black pepper	1 mL
1	clove garlic, pressed	1
4	whole leaves lettuce	4
	Few sprigs fresh coriander or parsley, chopped	

1. With a sharp knife, cut peel and pith away from whole grapefruits; cut on either side of membranes to release grapefruit segments. Put skinned grapefruit segments into a salad bowl. Scatter onions and olives over the grapefruit. Do not mix.

2. In a small bowl, whisk together olive oil, vinegar, lemon juice, paprika, salt, pepper and garlic until slightly emulsified. Drizzle dressing over grapefruit, onions and olives in the salad bowl. Fold gently, several times to mix ingredients and distribute the dressing. The salad can wait, covered and unrefrigerated, for up to 1 hour.

3. Place a lettuce leaf on each of 4 plates. Portion out the salad equally on top of the lettuce. Garnish with coriander and serve immediately.

Vegetable Side Dishes

Rapini with Balsamic Vinegar

Some of the healthiest vegetables are also the least popular — particularly bitter greens like dandelions and rapini. Why? Mostly because they are so often treated like spinach, steamed lightly and served either plain or buttered as a side vegetable. Done that way they taste like poison. To see how bitter greens can be made delicious we must look to the Italians, who use their unrivaled condiments and cheeses to create just the kind of culinary sorcery needed to make the greens pleasurable. These enhancements, which include olive oil, balsamic vinegar and Parmesan cheese, lend flavors and qualities that work with the bitterness and make it interesting.

✳ ✳ ✳

Tip

This salad can be served immediately, or it can wait, covered and unrefrigerated for up to 1 hour.

1	bunch rapini, washed, bottom 1 1/2 inches (4 cm) of stalks trimmed	1
1 tsp	salt	5 mL
3 tbsp	balsamic vinegar	45 mL
2 tbsp	extra virgin olive oil	25 mL
	Freshly ground black pepper to taste	
	Few sprigs fresh basil or parsley, chopped	
1/4 cup	thinly sliced red onion	50 mL
1 tsp	drained capers	5 mL
3 tbsp	shaved Parmesan or Pecorino cheese	45 mL

1. Prepare rapini. Cut off the top 2 1/2 inches (6 cm) — the part that has the leaves and the flowers — and set aside. Cut the remaining stalks into 1-inch (2.5 cm) pieces.

2. In a large pot, bring 1 1/2 inches (4 cm) of water to a boil. Add salt and chopped stalks and cook, uncovered, for 8 minutes, until tender. Add the reserved tops and cook, uncovered, for another 8 minutes. Drain, refresh with cold water, and drain again.

3. Transfer drained rapini to a serving plate and spread out. In a small bowl, combine vinegar, olive oil, pepper to taste and chopped basil or parsley. Evenly dress the rapini with this sauce. Scatter slices of red onion and capers over the rapini, and top with shaved cheese.

Stir-Fried Red Cabbage

SERVES 4 TO 6

Slightly tart, startlingly red-purple cabbage adds welcome sparkle and flavor (not to mention nutrition) to any vegetarian table. The fennel seeds and fresh dill add character without drawing away any of the assertiveness of the humble cabbage.

※ ※ ※

Tip

This dish can be served warm, or it can wait for up to 2 hours, covered and unrefrigerated, to be served at room temperature.

5½ cups	thinly shredded red cabbage	1.4 L
1 tbsp	cider vinegar	15 mL
1 tsp	salt	5 mL
2 tbsp	vegetable oil	25 mL
¼ tsp	salt	1 mL
¼ tsp	freshly ground black pepper	1 mL
1 tsp	whole fennel seeds	5 mL
1	small green bell pepper, cut into thin strips	1
1 tbsp	cider vinegar	15 mL
	Few sprigs fresh dill, chopped	

1. In a saucepan, cover cabbage with cold water; add vinegar and salt. Place on high heat for 7 to 8 minutes until just coming to a boil. Drain cabbage, refresh under cold water and drain again.

2. In a large frying pan, heat oil over high heat for 30 seconds. Add salt, pepper and fennel seeds and stir-fry for 1 minute, or until the seeds start to pop. Add green pepper strips and stir-fry for 1 minute until pepper wilts.

3. Add drained cabbage and stir-fry for 3 to 4 minutes until all the cabbage is shiny and warm through.

4. Remove from heat. Add cider vinegar and half of the chopped dill. Toss well to mix. Transfer to a serving dish and garnish with the remaining dill.

Jalapeño Broccoli

SERVES 4 TO 5

The stubby, lush green chilies that take their name from the Mexican city of Jalapa (in the state of Vera Cruz) have become as common in our markets as they are in their home country. Here is a recipe that uses their sweet heat to dress up therapeutic broccoli and actually makes it fun to eat.

✳ ✳ ✳

Tip
This salad can be served immediately or it can wait up to 2 hours, covered and unrefrigerated.

1 tsp	salt	5 mL
1	head broccoli, trimmed and separated into spears	1
1 tbsp	balsamic vinegar	15 mL
2 to 3 tbsp	olive oil	25 to 45 mL
2	fresh jalapeño peppers, thinly sliced (with or without seeds, depending on desired hotness)	2
¼ cup	toasted pine nuts Few sprigs fresh coriander or parsley, chopped	50 mL

1. Bring a pot of water to the boil and add salt. Add broccoli spears and boil over high heat for 3 to 5 minutes (depending on desired tenderness). Drain and transfer broccoli to bowl of ice cold water for 30 seconds. Drain and lay out the cooked spears decoratively on a presentation plate. Drizzle evenly with balsamic vinegar.

2. In a small frying pan, heat olive oil over medium heat for 30 seconds. Add sliced jalapeño peppers (with seeds, if using) and stir-fry for 2 to 3 minutes until softened. Take peppers with all the oil from the pan, and distribute evenly over broccoli. Garnish with pine nuts and herbs.

"Little" Broccoli Gratin

The "little" part of this recipe refers to a fine-chopping technique (borrowed from Daniaile's "Little" Cauliflower Salad, see page 87) that enhances the taste and texture of broccoli. The result combines crunchily boiled bits of broccoli with a number of zesty ingredients, all smothered in the lean mildness of melted bocconcini cheese and studded with toasted walnut pieces. It works well on its own and even better as a side dish to accompany broiled meat or chicken.

✳ ✳ ✳

Variation

If you wish, replace the bocconcini with the same weight of mozzarella nuggets — cut ¼ inch (0.5 cm) thick — for a slightly saltier result.

PREHEAT BROILER
10-INCH (25 CM) PIE PLATE OR BAKING DISH

1	bunch broccoli	1
2 tbsp	olive oil	25 mL
½ tsp	salt	2 mL
¼ tsp	freshly ground black pepper	1 mL
1 tbsp	minced fresh chili pepper or ¼ tsp (1 mL) hot pepper flakes	15 mL
1 cup	thickly sliced red onion	250 mL
8 oz	button mushrooms, trimmed and halved	250 g
1 tbsp	raisins	15 mL
1 tsp	white wine vinegar	5 mL
8 oz	bocconcini cheese, cut into ¼-inch (0.5 cm) rounds	250 g
½ cup	walnut pieces	125 mL

1. Separate florets of broccoli from the large stalks. (Reserve stalks for another use.) Chop florets into tiny match-head-sized bits. (You should get just over 2 cups/500 mL.) Bring a pot of salted water to a boil. Add broccoli; bring back to boil and cook for about 2 minutes. Drain through a fine wire strainer. Rinse under cold water; drain well and set aside.

2. In a large frying pan, heat oil, salt and pepper over high heat for 1 minute. Add chilies, onions and mushrooms; stir-fry for 3 minutes or until vegetables start to brown. Add raisins and vinegar; cook, stirring, for 30 seconds. Stir in broccoli; remove from heat.

3. Transfer contents of frying pan to a pie plate, spreading evenly to make a flat layer about ½ inch (1 cm) deep. Place rounds of bocconcini on top so that most of the surface is covered. Sprinkle the walnut pieces over the uncovered spots.

4. Broil 3 to 4 minutes until cheese is melted and walnuts have turned dark brown. Serve immediately in its baking dish to be portioned at table.

Bitter Greens with Paprika

SERVES 3 OR 4

Suitable as a starter or as a side dish with grilled or roasted meat, this hyper-nutritious dish has taste to spare. Here the bitterness of the main ingredient merges meaningfully with the various aromatics and condiments. A whole new dimension can be achieved by using non-bitter greens — like collard or kale — with exactly the same enhancements, making this an all-season recipe for the greens of your choice.

❋ ❋ ❋

1	bunch rapini or dandelion greens, washed, bottom 2 inches (5 cm) of stalks trimmed	1
2 tbsp	olive oil	25 mL
1 tsp	sweet paprika	5 mL
¼ tsp	turmeric	1 mL
¼ tsp	salt	1 mL
¼ tsp	freshly ground black pepper	1 mL
3	cloves garlic, thinly sliced	3
2 tbsp	freshly squeezed lemon juice	25 mL
1 tsp	drained capers	5 mL

1. Cut stalks of greens in half. Bring a pot of salted water to a boil and add the lower half of stalks. Let water return to boil and cook for 3 minutes. Add upper half of stalks (with the leaves); return to boil and cook for 3 minutes. Rinse under cold water; drain and set aside.

2. In a large frying pan, combine oil, paprika, turmeric, salt and pepper. Cook, stirring, over high heat for 1 minute. Add garlic; stir-fry for 30 seconds. Add drained greens; stir-fry for 2 minutes, folding from the bottom up to distribute garlic and spices evenly. Reduce heat to medium. Stir in lemon juice; cook, stirring, for 2 minutes. Stir in capers. Serve immediately.

Caraway Carrots

SERVES 4 TO 5

A modest recipe to enliven the lowly but highly nutritious carrot. For even more piquancy, use the fresh ginger. The butter can be replaced by vegetable oil but obviously butter is richer. If worried about calories, simply reduce the butter by half.

✳ ✳ ✳

3 cups	diagonally sliced carrots	750 mL
1 tsp	cornstarch	5 mL
1 tbsp	cold water	15 mL
2 tbsp	butter	25 mL
1 tbsp	whole caraway seeds	15 mL
1 tsp	grated gingerroot (optional)	5 mL
1 tbsp	honey, maple syrup or brown sugar	15 mL
1 tbsp	freshly squeezed lemon juice	15 mL
2	green onions, finely chopped	2

1. In a saucepan, cover carrot slices with cold water. Bring to a boil; cook 2 to 4 minutes, depending on desired tenderness. Drain carrots, reserving the cooking water.

2. In a small bowl, stir together cornstarch and water until dissolved.

3. In a deep saucepan, heat butter over medium heat until bubbling, about 1 or 2 minutes. Add caraway seeds and stir-fry for 1 to 2 minutes until the seeds begin to pop. Add ½ cup (125 mL) of the reserved cooking water, ginger, if using, and honey; cook, stirring occasionally, for 2 to 3 minutes, until nearly boiling. Stir dissolved cornstarch and add to sauce; reduce heat to low and cook, stirring, for 2 to 3 minutes until the sauce has the consistency of a thin syrup.

4. Fold carrots into the sauce and cook for 2 to 3 minutes until heated through. Remove from heat and stir in lemon juice. Transfer to a serving dish and garnish with green onions. Serve immediately.

Fennel Mushroom Stir-Fry

SERVES 4

*Bold, crunchy, colorful,
this simple stir-fry gains its
appeal from its large-chunk
vegetables and its simple
flavoring, which allows the
subtle licorice of the fennel
to shine through. It can be
enjoyed hot off the pan,
or at room temperature
on a party buffet.*

1	fennel bulb (about 1 lb/500 g)	1
3 tbsp	olive oil	45 mL
1/4 tsp	salt	1 mL
1/4 tsp	freshly ground black pepper	1 mL
1/2 cup	roughly chopped red onion	125 mL
1/2	red bell pepper, roughly chopped	1/2
2 1/2 cups	trimmed and halved mushrooms	625 mL
1 tbsp	freshly squeezed lemon juice	15 mL

1. Remove and discard any branches shooting up from the fennel bulb (they are fibrous and inedible). Cut the bulb in half, and trim away triangles of hard core. Chop remaining fennel in large chunks. Set aside.

2. In a large frying pan, heat olive oil over high heat for 30 seconds. Add salt, pepper, onions and red pepper. Stir-fry for 1 minute. Add fennel and stir-fry for 3 to 4 minutes, until the vegetables are slightly charred. Add mushrooms and stir-fry actively (the pan will be crowded by now) for 3 minutes, until mushrooms are slightly browned and soft. Remove from heat and stir in lemon juice. Transfer to a presentation dish and serve.

Grilled Eggplant with Goat Cheese (page 100)
Overleaf: Summer Artichoke Salad (page 86)

Cauliflower and Red Pepper

good ✓

VEGAN RECIPE

SERVES 6

A colorful, significantly dressed combination of lush red pepper and the oft-neglected cauliflower, this salad travels well on picnics in the summer, just as it helps to liven up a cozy dinner in winter. It is a particular favorite of Margaret Dragu, with whom I've shared many happy meals.

❊ ❊ ❊

1	head cauliflower, florets only	1
2	red bell peppers, roasted, skinned and cut into thick strips	2
1/4 tsp	salt	1 mL
1/4 tsp	freshly ground black pepper	1 mL
2 tbsp	freshly squeezed lemon juice	25 mL
1 tbsp	Dijon mustard	15 mL
1 tsp	vegetable oil	5 mL
1 tsp	black mustard seeds	5 mL
1/2 tsp	turmeric	2 mL
1/2 tsp	whole coriander seeds	2 mL
2	cloves garlic	2
2 tbsp	olive oil	25 mL

1/2 tsp Red Pepper

1. Blanch cauliflower florets in a large saucepan of boiling water for 5 to 6 minutes, until just cooked. Drain, refresh in iced water, drain again and transfer to a bowl. Add red peppers to cauliflower. Sprinkle with salt and pepper and toss.

2. In a small bowl, whisk together lemon juice and Dijon mustard until blended. Set aside.

3. In a small frying pan, heat vegetable oil over medium heat for 1 minute. Add mustard seeds, turmeric and coriander seeds, and stir-fry for 2 to 3 minutes, or until the seeds begin to pop. With a rubber spatula, scrape cooked spices from the pan into the lemon-mustard mixture. Squeeze garlic through a garlic press and add to the mixture. Add olive oil and whisk until the dressing has emulsified.

4. Add dressing to the cauliflower-red pepper mixture. Toss gently but thoroughly to dress all the pieces evenly. Transfer to a serving bowl, propping up the red pepper ribbons to properly accent the yellow-tinted cauliflower. This salad benefits greatly from a 1 or 2 hour wait, after which it should be served at room temperature.

Green Beans
with Cashews (page 103)

Wild Mushroom Fricassee with Rosemary

VEGAN RECIPE

SERVES 2

When it comes to appetizers, there's no ingredient to match wild mushrooms — meaty, lean, digestible and memorably delicious all at once. Here's a recipe with which to dazzle lovers and others (it can be easily multiplied as long as you use a large enough frying pan). It takes minutes to prepare and is also adaptable: You can make it with either red or white wine, whatever you happen to have on hand — just be sure to use the same color vinegar as your wine. You can use any kind of wild mushroom you prefer. Oyster and shiitakes can be used whole, trimmed of tough stalks. Portobellos must also be trimmed, then cut into slices 1/2 inch (1 cm) thick.

Tip

If your waistline allows, use an extra tablespoon (15 mL) butter at the beginning, as well as the optional teaspoon (5 mL) at the end, for a taste sensation worthy of the finest restaurant.

1 tbsp	butter (optional)	15 mL
1 tbsp	olive oil	15 mL
Pinch	freshly ground black pepper	Pinch
1 cup	thickly sliced red onion	250 mL
6 oz	wild mushrooms, trimmed	175 g
1 tbsp	minced garlic	15 mL
1 tbsp	finely chopped fresh rosemary or 1 tsp (5 mL) dried crumbled	15 mL
Pinch	salt	Pinch
1/2 tsp	white or red wine vinegar	2 mL
1/2 cup	white or red wine	125 mL
1 tsp	butter (optional)	5 mL
2	slices whole-wheat or black bread, toasted	2
	Few sprigs fresh parsley, chopped	

1. In a large nonstick frying pan, heat 1 tbsp (15 mL) butter, if using, oil and black pepper over high heat for 1 minute or until sizzling. Add onions and mushrooms; cook 3 to 4 minutes, turning every minute or so until they are nicely browned all over and have absorbed most of the liquid.
2. Add garlic and rosemary; stir-fry for 1 minute. Immediately add salt and vinegar; toss for a few seconds. Add wine and cook, shaking pan occasionally, for 2 to 3 minutes or until the sauce is thick and partially absorbed. Add 1 tsp (5 mL) butter, if using, and mix in until melted. Remove from heat.
3. Immediately cut the toasted bread diagonally into 4 pieces; arrange on 2 plates as toast points. Distribute mushrooms evenly in the middle of each plate and garnish with parsley. Serve immediately with a glass of the same wine you used in the recipe.

Stewed Okra

SERVES 4

A staple of Southern cooking, okra is the magical ingredient that can be used to thicken gumbo or, when breaded and deep fried, served as a crunchy snack. This okra recipe concentrates on the sweet-tart taste of okra itself.

2	medium tomatoes	2
1 lb	okra	500 g
2 tbsp	butter (optional)	25 mL
1 tbsp	olive oil	15 mL
1/2 tsp	hot pepper flakes	2 mL
4	cloves garlic, thinly sliced	4
1/2 tsp	freshly ground black pepper	2 mL
1 cup	water	250 mL
1 tbsp	lime juice	15 mL
1/2 tsp	salt	2 mL
	Few sprigs fresh coriander, chopped	

1. Blanch tomatoes in boiling water for 30 seconds. Over a bowl, peel, core and deseed them. Chop tomatoes into chunks and set aside. Strain any accumulated tomato juices from bowl; add the juices to the tomatoes.

2. With a sharp knife, trim 1/4 inch (0.5 cm) from the okra stems. Cut a vertical slit, 1 inch (2.5 cm) long, through the bellies of the okras, taking care not to slice them in half.

3. In a large frying pan, heat butter, if using, and oil over high heat until sizzling. Add hot pepper flakes and stir-fry for 30 seconds. Add okras and fry, actively tossing and turning for about 5 minutes, until they are scorched on both sides. Add garlic and black pepper; toss-fry for just under 1 minute until the garlic is frying (but before it burns).

4. Immediately add reserved tomato and tomato juice. Stir-fry for 1 minute until the tomato is beginning to fry. Add water and stir until it begins to boil around the okras. Reduce heat to simmer and cook for 20 minutes, gently folding and stirring every few minutes. (The okras will become increasingly tender and the sauce will thicken.)

5. Sprinkle okra with lime juice and salt. Gently fold and stir for under a minute and remove from heat. Transfer to a serving dish and garnish with chopped coriander. The okra can be served immediately but will improve if allowed to rest for about 30 minutes.

Grilled Eggplant with Goat Cheese

SERVES 4

This beautiful (if slightly calorific) dish takes a little while to prepare; but it can be done in two stages and is guaranteed to fetch compliments.

✳ ✳ ✳

Tip

In barbecue season, it is best to grill the eggplant slices instead of broiling them (Step 2). Grill 4 to 5 minutes on one side, turn over and grill another 3 minutes. You'll still need the broiler for the final gratin.

PREHEAT BROILER AND, IF USING, START BARBECUE (SEE TIP, LEFT)
BAKING SHEET

1	eggplant (about 1 lb/500 g)	1
1 tsp	salt	5 mL
2 tbsp	olive oil	25 mL
4 oz	soft goat cheese	125 g
1 tbsp	olive oil	15 mL
1 tbsp	balsamic vinegar	15 mL
1 tsp	drained capers	5 mL
	Freshly ground black pepper to taste	
	Few sprigs fresh basil and/or parsley, chopped	

1. Cut off top 1/2 inch (1 cm) of the eggplant and discard. Slice 12 perfect round slices, about 1/4 inch (0.5 cm) thick. Sprinkle salt on both sides of the eggplant slices, and let rest 10 minutes.

2. Rinse salt off the slices and pat dry. Brush each side of slices with the olive oil. Lay them out on a baking sheet and broil them 6 to 7 minutes on the first side, until soft. Flip them, and broil the second side for 2 to 3 minutes.

3. Remove from broiler. Arrange eggplant slices on the baking sheet in 4 clusters of 3 slices each. Divide the cheese into 4 equal portions and form each into a patty; place one patty in the center of each cluster. Sprinkle each cluster evenly with the olive oil.

4. Return to the broiler and broil for 2 to 3 minutes until the cheese is melted and has started to brown a little.

5. With a spatula, carefully lift each cluster onto a plate. Sprinkle with the vinegar, capers, black pepper and chopped herb(s). Serve immediately.

Summer Zucchini

SERVES 4

This is an ideal recipe for the vast quantities of lush, juicy zucchini we get every summer — mostly from all our friends with vegetable patches. Here I use young zucchini of both the yellow and green varieties, which, along with the red bell peppers, gives the dish additional color.

❄ ❄ ❄

4	young zucchini, preferably 2 each of green and yellow, less than 6 inches (15 cm) in length	4
3 tbsp	olive oil	45 mL
$\frac{1}{4}$ tsp	salt	1 mL
$\frac{1}{4}$ tsp	freshly ground black pepper	1 mL
1	red bell pepper, cut into thick strips	1
3	green onions, chopped	3
1 tbsp	freshly squeezed lemon juice	15 mL
	Few sprigs fresh basil and/or parsley, chopped	

1. Trim ends of zucchini and cut into $\frac{3}{4}$-inch (2 cm) chunks. Set aside.

2. In a large frying pan, heat olive oil over high heat for 30 seconds. Add salt and pepper and stir. Add zucchini chunks and red pepper strips. Stir-fry for 4 to 6 minutes until the zucchini have browned on both sides and the red pepper has softened. Add green onions and stir-fry for 30 seconds. Transfer to a serving dish and drizzle evenly with lemon juice. Garnish with basil and/or parsley and serve immediately.

Zucchini Algis

**SERVES 2 AS A MAIN
COURSE OR 4 AS
AN APPETIZER**

*Photographer Algis Kemezys,
my longtime partner and
sous-chef, invented this
simple yet satisfying dish as
a vegetarian main course for
Chez Byron, our Montreal
restaurant. It also works
wonderfully on its own as a
summer appetizer or side
dish to accompany any
main course.*

❋ ❋ ❋

1	tomato	1
1/4 cup	olive oil	50 mL
1/4 tsp	salt	1 mL
1/4 tsp	freshly ground black pepper	1 mL
3 cups	diagonally sliced zucchini	750 mL
1	onion, sliced	1
1 3/4 cups	thickly sliced mushrooms	425 mL
2 to 3	cloves garlic, thinly sliced	2 to 3
2 tbsp	white wine or water	25 mL
	Few sprigs fresh basil and/or dill, chopped	

1. Blanch tomato in boiling water for 30 seconds. Over a bowl, peel, core and deseed it. Chop tomato into chunks and set aside. Strain any accumulated tomato juices from bowl; add the juices to the tomato.

2. In a large frying pan, heat olive oil on high heat for 30 seconds. Add salt and pepper and stir. Add zucchini and onions. Stir-fry for 3 to 4 minutes, until the zucchini is slightly charred.

3. Add mushroom slices and continue stir-frying (gently, so as not to injure the zucchini) for 2 to 3 minutes. Add garlic and stir-fry for 1 minute. Add reserved tomato and its juice, and stir-fry for 2 to 3 minutes until a sauce begins to form.

4. Remove from heat and stir in wine. You should have a spare but luscious sauce. Transfer to a serving dish and garnish with the basil and/or dill. Serve immediately.

Green Beans with Cashews

SERVES 4

The simple addition of cashews and red onions to this dish transforms ordinary green beans into a formidable companion to any gourmet main course.

1 lb	green beans, trimmed	500 g
2 tbsp	olive oil	25 mL
$\frac{1}{2}$ cup	slivered red onion	125 mL
$\frac{1}{3}$ cup	raw cashews	75 mL
$\frac{1}{4}$ tsp	salt	1 mL
$\frac{1}{4}$ tsp	freshly ground black pepper	1 mL
	Few sprigs fresh parsley, chopped	

1. Blanch green beans in a pot of boiling water for 5 minutes. Drain and immediately refresh in a bowl of ice-cold water. Drain and set aside.

2. In a large frying pan, heat olive oil over medium-high heat for 30 seconds. Add onions, cashews, salt and pepper and stir-fry for 2 to 3 minutes, until the onions are softened. Add cooked green beans, increase heat to high, and stir-fry actively for 2 to 3 minutes, until the beans feel hot to the touch. (Take care that you don't burn any cashews in the process.) Transfer to a serving plate and garnish with chopped parsley. Serve immediately.

Green Beans and Tomato

SERVES 4 TO 6

These slow-simmered green beans belong to that group of oily, overcooked vegetables the Greeks call lathera (literally, "cooked in oil"). Given contemporary preferences for super-crunchy, sparsely sauced vegetables, they may seem seriously retro. But they offer their own reward. Mushy and saucy, these are the beans I grew up with in my mother's Greek kitchen, and it took me years to appreciate any other type.

✹ ✹ ✹

Tip

These beans can be made up to 2 hours ahead, then kept covered and unrefrigerated.

1 tbsp	tomato paste	15 mL
1 cup	warm water	250 mL
1/4 cup	olive oil	50 mL
1/4 tsp	salt	1 mL
1/4 tsp	freshly ground black pepper	1 mL
2	medium onions, sliced	2
1	sweet or hot banana pepper	1
4	cloves garlic, thinly sliced	4
2	medium tomatoes, cut into thick wedges	2
1 tsp	granulated sugar	5 mL
	Few sprigs fresh parsley, roughly chopped	
1 lb	green beans, trimmed	500 g

1. In a small bowl, stir together tomato paste and water until dissolved. Set aside.

2. In a large, heavy-bottomed saucepan, heat olive oil over high heat for about 1 minute. Add salt, pepper and onions. Stir-fry for 2 minutes, until onions are softened. Add whole banana pepper and stir-fry for 1 minute. Add garlic and stir-fry for 30 seconds.

3. Add tomato wedges (skin and seeds are all right for this recipe) and stir-cook for 1 to 2 minutes until softened. Add the dissolved tomato paste, sugar, and most of the parsley (reserve some parsley for the final garnish). Stir-cook for 1 to 2 minutes until contents are bubbling. Add green beans and stir, immersing the beans in the sauce until it has come back to a boil, about 30 seconds. Reduce heat to medium-low and simmer, uncovered, for 30 to 40 minutes, stirring occasionally, until the beans have lost 90% of their crunch.

4. Using tongs, transfer beans to a serving bowl, leaving behind as much of the sauce as possible. Increase heat to high and boil sauce until reduced to a syrupy consistency, about 5 to 7 minutes. If the sauce becomes too thick, add some water and bring back to boil. Pour sauce evenly over the beans. Garnish with the remaining parsley and serve.

Mushroom and Green Bean Stir-Fry

SERVES 4

Mixing and matching vegetables to create delicious combinations is an age-old culinary trick to get healthy food on the table. The appeal of this one is derived from the crunchy mushrooms, which contrast so nicely with the tenderness of the green beans. The whole lot is enhanced by the aromatics and lemon juice. It makes for a light starter, or a perfect accompaniment to grilled meat or fish in a main course.

✳ ✳ ✳

8 oz	green beans, trimmed and halved	250 g
4 oz	carrots, scraped and sliced into ¼-inch (0.5 cm) rounds	125 g
¼ cup	olive oil	50 mL
8 oz	mushrooms, trimmed and cut into ½-inch (1 cm) chunks	250 g
5	cloves garlic, thinly sliced	5
3	sun-dried tomatoes, thinly sliced	3
½ tsp	salt	2 mL
¼ tsp	freshly ground black pepper	1 mL
2 tbsp	freshly squeezed lemon juice	25 mL
½ cup	white wine	125 mL
4	canned artichoke hearts, drained and cut into quarters	4
⅓ cup	roasted pine nuts	75 mL
	Extra virgin olive oil for drizzling (optional)	

1. Bring a pot of salted water to a boil. Add green beans and carrots; let water return to a boil and cook 5 minutes. Rinse under plenty of cold water; drain and set aside.

2. In a large frying pan, heat oil over high heat for 1 minute. Add mushrooms and cook, stirring actively, 3 minutes until golden brown on all sides (they will absorb all or most of the oil). Add garlic, sun-dried tomatoes, salt and pepper; stir-fry for 1 minute.

3. Immediately add lemon juice and let it sizzle for 1 minute. Stir in wine; bring to a boil and cook, stirring, for 1 minute. Reduce heat to medium-high. Add beans and carrots; cook, stirring, for 2 minutes. Add artichoke hearts; cook, stirring, for 3 minutes. Serve immediately, garnished with pine nuts and olive oil, if desired, on the side for drizzling at table.

Braised Green Beans and Fennel

SERVES 4 TO 6

Here's another healthy and interesting way to serve up Mediterranean-style vegetables. In this recipe we forego boiling in favor of a quick stir-fry followed by 20 minutes of braising and simmering. The result is a comfortingly soft, yet still crunchy texture, and a pleasing licorice flavor. The recipe works beautifully as a warm-up starter salad, or as a side vegetable to grilled meat or fish. Green beans provide the bulk, but it is the fresh fennel that gives it character.

✳ ✳ ✳

Tip

The fennel bulb always comes attached to woody branches and thin leaves that look like dill. You'll need the leaves for the final garnish, so cut them off and set them aside. Cut off and discard the woody branches. Quarter the bulb vertically, then cut out and discard the hard triangular sections of core. What remains is the usable part of the fennel.

¼ cup	olive oil	50 mL
½ tsp	salt	2 mL
¼ tsp	freshly ground black pepper	1 mL
1 tsp	whole fennel seeds	5 mL
12 oz	green beans, trimmed	375 g
1	large or 2 small fennel bulbs, trimmed, cored, and cut into ½-inch (1 cm) slices (see Tip, left)	1
1	small carrot, scraped and sliced into ¼-inch (0.5 cm) rounds	1
6	cloves garlic, thinly sliced	6
1 cup	water	250 mL
1 tbsp	balsamic vinegar	15 mL
	Few sprigs fennel greens, chopped	

1. In a large, deep frying pan, heat olive oil, salt and pepper over high heat for 1 minute. Add fennel seeds; stir-fry 1 minute or until just browning. Add green beans, fennel and carrots; stir-fry 3 minutes or until all the vegetables are shiny and beginning to sizzle. Add garlic; stir-fry for 1 more minute.

2. Immediately add water and vinegar; cook 2 minutes or until bubbling. Reduce heat to medium-low, cover pan tightly and cook 20 minutes.

3. Place a strainer over a bowl and strain contents of the pan. Transfer the strained vegetables onto a platter and keep warm. Transfer the liquid that has collected in the bowl back into the pan; bring to a boil and cook 6 to 7 minutes or until thick and syrupy.

4. Spoon the reduced sauce over the vegetables, garnish with the chopped fennel greens and serve immediately.

Herbed Potatoes

SERVES 4

When the palate demands the wonderful taste of fried potatoes, but the waistline says "no" to French fries, try this zesty re-fry of parboiled potato. It uses a minimum of oil, and delivers delightful flavors.

1 lb	new potatoes, unpeeled but well scrubbed (about 3)	500 g
¼ cup	olive oil	50 mL
¼ tsp	salt	1 mL
¼ tsp	freshly ground black pepper	1 mL
1 tbsp	grated lemon zest	15 mL
4	cloves garlic, finely chopped	4
	Few sprigs fresh parsley and/or rosemary, chopped	
2 tbsp	freshly squeezed lemon juice	25 mL

1. In a large saucepan, boil potatoes over high heat for 5 to 7 minutes, until they can just be pierced with a fork. Drain and refresh several times with cold water. Cut potatoes into ½-inch (1 cm) rounds.

2. In a large frying pan, heat oil over high heat for 30 seconds. Add salt and pepper and stir. Add potatoes in a single layer and fry for 2 to 3 minutes; reduce heat to medium-high, turn rounds over and fry other side for 2 to 3 minutes, then toss-fry for another 1 to 2 minutes until golden all over. (Some of the skins will have peeled off and fried to a crisp; don't worry, they'll add to the final appeal.)

3. Add lemon zest, garlic and most of the chopped herb(s), reserving some for the final garnish. Toss-fry for 1 to 2 minutes. Add lemon juice and toss-fry for 1 to 2 minutes until the sizzle has stopped and the acidity of the lemon has mellowed. (Taste a piece.) Transfer potatoes to a serving bowl and garnish with the remainder of the herb(s). Serve immediately.

Grilled Leeks with Feta and Red Pepper

SERVES 4

It is rumored that the laborers who built the pyramids of ancient Egypt survived primarily on leeks (cooked in honey, but that's another story). If true, that tidbit of leek-lore should put this oniony, versatile vegetable in league with Popeye's spinach. Its superpowers aside, the leek is a lovely vegetable and easy to deal with, if certain care is taken — especially with cleaning. The final presentation of this recipe depends for its beauty on the leek being cooked (using two separate techniques consecutively) with its stem intact so that it can stay in one long, graceful piece. The slit required in Step 1 is also tricky, since it has to be wide and deep enough to allow cleaning but without slicing right through.

✻ ✻ ✻

PREHEAT BROILER
13-BY 9-INCH (3 L) BAKING DISH

4	leeks (about 1 lb/500 g)	4
1/4 cup	olive oil, divided	50 mL
1	red bell pepper, trimmed and quartered	1
4 oz	feta cheese, crumbled	125 g
1 tbsp	red wine vinegar	15 mL
1/4 tsp	freshly ground black pepper	1 mL
4	black olives, pitted and chopped	4

1. To ensure that leeks do not separate, make a vertical 3-inch (7.5 cm) slit through the middle of each leek. Wash sand away from central layers (where the white and green meet) through this slit. Bring a large pot of salted water to a boil. Add leeks; cook 6 to 8 minutes or until tender and easily pierceable. Drain. Rinse with cold water; drain.

2. Spread 1 tbsp (15 mL) of the olive oil in the bottom of baking dish. Transfer leeks onto oil and straighten them to their original length. Roll them in the oil, ending with the slit-side up. Fit the red pepper quarters into the corners of the pan and roll, coating both sides in the oil, ending with skin-side up. Mound one-quarter of the feta crumbles into the slit cavity of each leek and spread it out to cover the length of the slit. (The recipe can be prepared to this point and kept up to 1 hour, covered and unrefrigerated.)

3. Broil leeks under a hot broiler for 7 to 10 minutes or until feta is browned and peppers are quite charred.

4. Immediately (and carefully) lift each leek and curl it on a plate, feta-side up. Lift red peppers off the oven dish and cut them roughly into bite-size bits. Distribute bits inside semi-circles of leek on each plate. In a small bowl, whisk together remaining olive oil, red wine vinegar and black pepper. Drizzle about 1 tbsp (15 mL) of this dressing over vegetables on each plate. Garnish the feta surface of the leeks with olive bits and serve immediately while still warm.

Potato and Leek Avgolemono

SERVES 4

This dish features slow-braised leek with potato and carrot, in a simple but delightful sauce. It takes you back to a time of rustic pleasures and leisurely dining. Warning: the sauce of this dish is so tempting, you'll find yourself sopping it up with bread, refined sensibility or table manners notwithstanding.

❈ ❈ ❈

4	leeks (about 1 lb/500 g)	4
1/4 cup	olive oil	50 mL
1/4 tsp	salt	1 mL
1/4 tsp	freshly ground black pepper	1 mL
2 cups	cubed potatoes	500 mL
3/4 cup	sliced carrots	175 mL
1 cup	water	250 mL
1	egg	1
2 tbsp	freshly squeezed lemon juice	25 mL

1. To ensure that leeks do not completely separate, make a vertical 3-inch (7.5 cm) slit through the middle of each leek. Wash sand away from central layers (where the white and green meet) through this slit. Now cut off the hairy stem and discard. Slice the rest of the leek (green and white parts alike) into 1 1/2-inch (4 cm) chunks. Set aside.

2. In a large saucepan, heat oil over high heat for 1 minute. Add salt and pepper and stir. Add leeks, potatoes and carrots. Gently stir-fry for 2 to 3 minutes until ingredients are well coated with oil, but without charring the leeks. Add water and stir gently to mix. Let it come to a boil then reduce heat to low, cover and braise for 20 to 25 minutes, until all the vegetables are easily pierced with a fork.

3. Using a slotted spoon, transfer the cooked vegetables to a serving dish, leaving behind as much of the liquid as possible. Increase heat to high and boil down the liquid for 1 to 2 minutes, until reduced by about 30%.

4. In a bowl, whisk egg and lemon juice together. Add 1 tbsp (15 mL) of the hot cooking liquid and vigorously whisk into the egg. Repeat 3 or 4 more times, whisking in a tablespoon (15 mL) at a time, then add the rest of the liquid in a thin stream, whisking all the while. Pour sauce evenly over the vegetables, and serve within 30 minutes.

Romano Bean Stew

VEGAN RECIPE

SERVES 4 TO 6

Lovers of hot food will enjoy this combination of spicy sauce, sweetly plump romano beans and fried almonds. It is best served with other spicy dishes, but it works wonderfully to perk up simple meals of rice and plain vegetables.

Tip

For romano beans you can either cook your own, or use canned. A 19-oz (540 mL) can of romano beans, rinsed and drained, will yield exactly the 2 cups (500 mL) you'll need for this recipe.

2	medium tomatoes	2
1/4 cup	olive oil	50 mL
1/2 tsp	salt	2 mL
1 tsp	whole cumin seeds	5 mL
2	onions, sliced	2
1	fresh jalapeño pepper, diced (with or without seeds, depending on desired hotness)	1
1/2 cup	water	125 mL
1 tbsp	raisins	15 mL
2 cups	cooked romano beans (see Tip, left)	500 mL
1 tbsp	olive oil	15 mL
1/2 cup	slivered almonds	125 mL

1. Blanch tomatoes in boiling water for 30 seconds. Over a bowl, peel, core and deseed them. Chop tomatoes into chunks and set aside. Strain any accumulated tomato juices from bowl; add the juices to the tomatoes.
2. In a deep frying pan, heat olive oil over high heat for 1 minute. Add salt and cumin seeds and stir-fry for 1 minute. Add onions and stir-fry for 2 minutes until softened. Add jalapeño pepper (and seeds, if desired). Stir-fry for 1 to 2 minutes, until ingredients are well coated and starting to char.
3. Add reserved tomato and juices. Stir-fry for 2 to 3 minutes until tomatoes are breaking up. Add water and let it come back to boil. Stir in raisins, then fold in beans. Reduce heat to medium-low and simmer for 5 minutes, stirring occasionally to prevent scorching. Transfer to a serving bowl.
4. In a frying pan, heat oil over high heat for 30 seconds. Add slivered almonds and fry for 1 to 2 minutes, stirring and turning constantly until browned. Take off heat and immediately transfer to a cool dish. Scatter almonds on top of beans. This dish will be at its best if allowed to rest for 1 or 2 hours, then served at room temperature.

Yahni (Greek Beans with Onions)

SERVES 6

The affinity of beans to onions is no culinary secret, but this heirloom recipe stretches the notion to its limits. A mixture of approximately equal amounts of onion to beans, it is further onion-enhanced with a garnish of raw onion at the end. It results in a sweet, satisfyingly flavored bean dish that can be used on the side of any Mediterranean main course.

✿ ✿ ✿

Tip

If using canned kidney beans, a 19-oz (540 mL) can of beans, rinsed and drained, will yield 2 cups (500 mL) required for this recipe.

2	medium tomatoes	2
1/4 cup	olive oil	50 mL
1/4 tsp	salt	1 mL
1/4 tsp	freshly ground black pepper	1 mL
2 cups	thinly sliced onion	500 mL
1	stick celery, finely diced	1
4	cloves garlic, thinly sliced	4
1 cup	water	250 mL
1/4 cup	chopped fresh parsley, packed down	50 mL
1 tbsp	red wine vinegar	15 mL
1 tsp	granulated sugar	5 mL
2 cups	cooked white kidney beans (see Tip, left)	500 mL
	Extra virgin olive oil, to taste	
1/4 cup	finely diced red onion	50 mL

1. Blanch tomatoes in boiling water for 30 seconds. Over a bowl, peel, core and deseed them. Chop tomatoes into chunks and set aside. Strain any accumulated tomato juices from bowl; add the juices to the tomatoes.

2. In a large frying pan, heat oil over high heat for 30 seconds. Add salt and pepper and stir. Add onions and celery and stir-fry for 5 minutes until wilted. Add garlic and stir-fry for 1 minute, until garlic is well coated with oil and everything is shiny.

3. Add tomato and its juices. Stir-fry for 2 minutes, mixing well. Add water, parsley, vinegar and sugar; bring back to a boil. Reduce heat to medium-low and cook for 5 to 6 minutes. Stir occasionally, mashing the tomato until it has broken down and the sauce is pink.

4. Fold beans into the sauce. Cook 5 to 6 minutes, stirring occasionally (and gently), until most of the liquid has been absorbed and everything is well integrated.

5. Transfer to a serving dish. Drizzle with virgin olive oil and top with red onions. Let rest covered and unrefrigerated for 1 to 2 hours to develop flavor. Serve at room temperature.

Mushrooms Provençale

SERVES 4 TO 6

These quick-to-fry mushrooms are wholesome as a side course, and satisfy wonderfully as an appetizer on their own. The key to success here is searing the mushrooms over very high heat, sealing in their moisture, but without burning them. If properly made, they'll be succulent even when cold and therefore can be enjoyed at a buffet lunch or dinner.

Tip

The mushrooms can be served immediately (when they are at their best), or they can wait up to 2 hours, covered and unrefrigerated.

¼ cup	olive oil	50 mL
¼ tsp	freshly ground black pepper	1 mL
1 lb	mushrooms, trimmed	500 g
4	cloves garlic, finely chopped	4
2 tbsp	freshly squeezed lemon juice	25 mL
	Salt to taste	
	Few sprigs fresh parsley, chopped	

1. In a large frying pan, heat olive oil over high heat for 1 minute. Add black pepper and mushrooms. Stir-fry for 2 to 3 minutes, turning the mushrooms often to sear them on all sides without burning them.

2. Add garlic and stir-fry 1 minute. Remove from heat; stir in lemon juice and salt to taste. Transfer mushrooms and sauce to a serving dish and garnish with chopped parsley.

Lentils-Rice-Spinach

SERVES 4 TO 6

This is a variation of spanakorizo (spinach-rice), a rustic winter staple of the eastern Mediterranean, where spinach is one of the leafy vegetables that keep growing in the cold months. The lentils are my own addition, but they are in keeping with the traditions of this kind of cuisine. They also bolster this dish into main-course status.

✳ ✳ ✳

Tip
The lentils-rice-spinach can be served immediately, or it can wait for up to 2 hours, covered and unrefrigerated.

¼ cup	olive oil	50 mL
¼ tsp	salt	1 mL
¼ tsp	freshly ground black pepper	1 mL
2 cups	diced onion	500 mL
1	medium tomato, cubed	1
4 cups	chopped fresh spinach leaves, packed down	1 L
1½ cups	cooked rice (½ cup/125 mL uncooked rice)	375 mL
2 cups	cooked green lentils	500 mL
1	lemon, cut into wedges	1

1. In a pot or large skillet, heat oil over high heat for 30 seconds. Add salt and pepper and stir for 30 seconds. Add onions and stir-fry for 2 minutes until softened. Add cubed tomato and stir-fry for 1 minute.

2. Add all the spinach at once; cook, turning over several times, until spinach has been reduced to one-third of its volume, about 1 minute.

3. Reduce heat to medium-low and add rice and lentils. Stir-cook for 3 to 4 minutes, until well mixed and everything is piping hot. Remove from heat, cover and let rest for 5 to 6 minutes as it develops flavor. Serve with lemon wedges on the side.

Spinach Florentine

SERVES 4

*A spinach recipe for those
who prefer their vitamins
and Popeye-like strength
from palate teasers. Perked
up with garlic and sun-dried
tomato and mantled with
two kinds of cheese, this
bundle of tasty greens is as
irresistible as it is nutritious.*

❋ ❋ ❋

Variation

This dish can be turned
into Eggs Florentine —
the café-brunch fave
— if served under
poached or fried eggs.
This quantity of spinach
can cater to 2 large
appetites if split in half
and served with 2 eggs
each, or 4 modest ones
if divided into quarters
with an egg atop
each serving.

1 cup	water	250 mL
¹⁄₂ tsp	salt	2 mL
4 cups	finely chopped fresh spinach, packed down	1 L
2 tbsp	olive oil	25 mL
¹⁄₄ tsp	salt	1 mL
¹⁄₄ tsp	freshly ground black pepper	1 mL
3	cloves garlic, finely chopped	3
3	sun-dried tomatoes, finely sliced	3
2 tbsp	chopped fresh tarragon or 1 tsp (5 mL) dried	25 mL
1 cup	shredded mozzarella cheese	250 mL
1 tbsp	grated Parmesan cheese	15 mL

1. In a large saucepan, bring water to a rolling boil over high heat. Add salt. Add spinach, cover, and cook for 2 minutes until spinach has greatly reduced in volume and is bright green. Drain and refresh with cold water. (Let drain on its own, without pressing down.)

2. In a large frying pan, heat olive oil over high heat for 30 seconds. Add salt, pepper and garlic; stir-fry for 30 seconds. Add sun-dried tomatoes and stir-fry for another 30 seconds. Add spinach and tarragon, and stir-fry for 1 minute, folding the ingredients together. Reduce heat to medium.

3. Spread spinach out over bottom of pan. Sprinkle evenly with mozzarella and Parmesan. Cover pan and let cook until cheese melts, about 1 to 2 minutes. Remove from heat and keep covered. Serve as soon as possible.

Dishes for Entertaining

Olive Oil Crust

**MAKES 4
SMALL CRUSTS**

*This is an all-purpose crust
for savory pies, and serves
as a serious competitor
to store-bought phyllo.
It is easy to work with:
trimmings can be re-rolled
with no loss, and it lives
happily in the fridge for up
to five days. It can also be
frozen, but must be fully
defrosted, and the oil that
will have seeped out must be
worked back into the dough.*

1³⁄4 cups	all-purpose flour	425 mL
1 ¹⁄2 tsp	salt	7 mL
1 ¹⁄2 tsp	baking powder	7 mL
¹⁄2 cup	olive oil	125 mL
¹⁄2 cup	milk	125 mL
1	egg, beaten	1
	Additional flour, as needed	

1. In a bowl, sift together flour, salt and baking powder. In a separate bowl, whisk together olive oil, milk and beaten egg. Add the liquid ingredients all at once to the dry ingredients. Using fingers or an electric mixer with dough hook, blend the liquids into the flour. (If you use a mixer, scrape down the sides of the bowl several times.) This shouldn't take long; the dough will have absorbed the liquids and have the texture of an earlobe. If dough does not have the correct texture, work in another 2 tbsp (25 mL) flour.

2. Transfer dough to a storage bowl, cover and refrigerate for at least ¹⁄2 hour. When ready to use, knead any oil that may have seeped out back into the dough.

3. To roll crusts for making the pies in this book, divide the dough into 4 equal pieces. On a floured work surface, take one of the pieces of dough and flatten it into a round with your hand. Turn it over to flour the other side. Using a floured rolling pin, roll dough into a round sheet about 8 or 9 inches (20 or 22 cm) in diameter and about ¹⁄8 inch (0.2 cm) thick. It will shrink a little on its own, but can be stretched by hand later. Transfer onto a piece of waxed paper. Repeat procedure for each of the 3 remaining pieces of dough, and stack them, separated by waxed paper, to ensure that they peel off easily when ready to use. The stack can then be covered and refrigerated.

Spinach Feta Pie

SERVES 4 FOR DINNER; UP TO 16 FOR SNACKS

Unarguably the most famous of Greek savories, spinach pie (spanakopita) is enjoyed the world over. This recipe deviates slightly from tradition with its use of raw spinach and leeks, making for a crunchier, fresher-tasting pie.

✻ ✻ ✻

Tips

The pies are served hot from the oven, but are just as tasty at room temperature.

For a main course, serve an entire pie per person, accompanied by Cucumber Raita (see recipe, page 167) and a salad; as an appetizer, slice each pie into quarters and serve on a platter.

PREHEAT OVEN TO 400°F (200°C)
BAKING SHEET, GREASED LIGHTLY WITH VEGETABLE OIL

4 cups	finely chopped fresh spinach, packed down	1 L
2 cups	finely chopped leek, white and green parts alike, packed	500 mL
1 cup	crumbled feta cheese	250 mL
1 cup	grated mozzarella cheese	250 mL
3 tbsp	currants or raisins	45 mL
2 tbsp	chopped fresh dill or 1 tsp (5 mL) dried	25 mL
2 tbsp	chopped fresh parsley	25 mL
1/2 tsp	freshly ground black pepper	2 mL
2	eggs	2
1 tsp	cornstarch	5 mL
4	sheets Olive Oil Crust (see recipe, page 116)	4
1	egg	1
1 tbsp	milk	15 mL

1. In a bowl, combine spinach, leeks, feta, mozzarella, currants, dill, parsley and black pepper; mix well. Beat together eggs and cornstarch; add to spinach mixture and stir to mix thoroughly.

2. On a floured surface, lay out sheet of olive oil crust. Spoon one-quarter of the spinach mixture (about 1 1/2 cups/375 mL) onto the lower half of the crust. Fold the upper half over and, with your fingers or fork, pinch the edges together. Place pie on prepared baking sheet. Repeat procedure with the other three pies. Beat the egg and milk together and brush over the crusts. Bake in preheated oven for 20 to 22 minutes, until golden brown and crusty. Pick pies off the pan with a metal spatula, cutting off any yellow, eggy fluff that may have leaked during the baking. Serve immediately.

Individual Vegetable Goat Cheese Pie

SERVES 4

Filling and heartwarming, here's a dish for those lazy Sundays that get capped with a special meal. Timewise, the crust can be made ahead, and the filling will take about 45 minutes, after which it can wait a couple of hours, covered and unrefrigerated. The final assembly and baking takes about a half hour. Calories? On a lazy Sunday, who's counting?

❋ ❋ ❋

PREHEAT OVEN TO 400°F (200°C)
4 RAMEKINS, 1½ CUP (375 mL) CAPACITY, MEASURING 1 TO 2 INCHES (2.5 TO 5 CM) DEEP AND 5 INCHES (12.5 CM) WIDE

1 lb	ripe tomatoes (about 4)	500 g
8 oz	potatoes, unpeeled but scrubbed	250 g
5 tbsp	olive oil, divided	75 mL
½ tsp	salt	2 mL
½ tsp	freshly ground black pepper	2 mL
2½ cups	zucchini, thinly sliced	625 mL
1½ cups	chopped onion	375 mL
½ cup	chopped green peppers	125 mL
3 cups	sliced mushrooms	750 mL
5	cloves garlic, finely chopped	5
1 tsp	dried oregano leaves	5 mL
1½ tsp	tomato paste	7 mL
¾ cup	hot water	175 mL
4 oz	soft goat cheese	125 g
4	sheets Olive Oil Crust (see recipe, page 116)	4
1	egg	1
1 tbsp	milk	15 mL

1. Blanch tomatoes in boiling water for 30 seconds. Over a bowl, peel, core and deseed them. Chop tomatoes roughly and set aside. Strain any accumulated tomato juices from bowl and add to tomato pieces.

2. Boil potato for 6 or 7 minutes, just until it can be pierced with a fork. Let cool for a few minutes, and cut into ½-inch (1 cm) cubes. Set aside.

3. In a large frying pan, heat ¼ cup (50 mL) of the olive oil on high heat for 30 seconds. Add salt and pepper and stir for 30 seconds. Add potato cubes and fry, turning for 5 minutes, until browned and soft. Transfer potatoes to a bowl.

4. In the frying pan, fry zucchini slices, turning, for 3 or 4 minutes until browned. Remove and add to reserved potatoes.

5. Heat remaining olive oil. Add onions and green peppers; stir-fry for 2 to 3 minutes. Add mushrooms and stir-fry for 1 to 2 minutes. Add garlic and stir-fry for 1 to 2 minutes.

6. Add tomato flesh and juices and oregano to the pan. Stir-cook for 3 minutes to break up the tomato somewhat. Add tomato paste diluted in hot water and reduce heat to medium. Stir-cook 3 to 4 minutes, until everything is integrated and bubbling. Add the contents of the frying pan to the bowl with the potatoes and zucchini. Mix well to integrate.

7. Put one-quarter of the vegetable mixture (about 1¼ cups/300 mL) into each ramekin, making sure that every portion has some liquid. Divide the goat cheese into 4 pieces, and flatten each piece into a 2-inch (5 cm) disk. Place one disk on top of each pie.

8. Cover the filling and cheese with a sheet of crust, pinching the excess pastry to the outside edges of rims. Beat the egg and milk together and brush all over the crusts.

9. Bake in preheated oven for 20 to 22 minutes, until pie crusts are golden brown. Serve immediately with salad.

Leek-Potato-Lentil Pie

SERVES 4

The subtly flavored filling of this pie highlights the sweet, earthy tastes of its main ingredients. It is made with no dairy products at all, and can be enjoyed vegan-style with an accompaniment of Mango-Cucumber Salad, although the yogurt-based Cucumber Raita adds several layers of luxury.

❋ ❋ ❋

Tip

Be sure to wash leeks thoroughly, splitting down the middle and paying special care to the grit that hides where the green and white parts meet.

PREHEAT OVEN TO 400°F (200°C)
4 RAMEKINS, 1½ CUP (375 mL) CAPACITY, MEASURING 1 TO 2 INCHES (2.5 TO 5 CM) DEEP AND 5 INCHES (12.5 CM) WIDE

¼ cup	olive oil	50 mL
¼ tsp	salt	1 mL
¼ tsp	freshly ground black pepper	1 mL
8 oz	boiled potatoes, cubed (about 2)	250 g
2	leeks, green and white parts alike, finely chopped (see Tip, left)	2
½ cup	Tomato Sauce (see recipe, page 138)	125 mL
1½ cups	tomato juice	375 mL
2 cups	cooked lentils	500 mL
1 cup	thinly shredded spinach, packed	250 mL
¼ cup	finely chopped fresh parsley	50 mL
4	sheets Olive Oil Crust (see recipe, page 116)	4
1	egg	1
1 tbsp	milk	15 mL
	Mango-Cucumber Salad (see recipe, page 82)	
	Cucumber Raita (see recipe, page 167)	

1. In a large, deep frying pan, heat olive oil over high heat. Add salt and pepper and stir. Add potatoes and leeks. Actively stir-fry until leeks have cooked down to one-quarter of their original volume, about 5 minutes.

2. Add tomato sauce and tomato juice; stir to bring back to boil. Reduce heat to medium. Add lentils and cook, stirring, for 5 minutes until everything is piping hot and well mixed. Add chopped spinach, turn a few times and transfer mixture to a bowl. Add chopped parsley and mix in. Let mixture cool down for about 20 minutes, uncovered and unrefrigerated.

3. Put one-quarter of the mixture (about $1\frac{1}{4}$ cups/300 mL) into each ramekin. Cover the filling with a sheet of crust, pinching the excess pastry to the outside edges of rims. Whisk together egg and milk and brush over the crusts. Bake in preheated oven for 20 to 22 minutes, until golden brown and crusty. Serve with Mango Cucumber Salad, and/or Cucumber Raita.

Eggplant and Mushroom Pie

SERVES 4 AS A MAIN COURSE; UP TO 16 AS AN APPETIZER

The earthy taste and slithery texture of eggplant and mushroom combine in this pattie-like pie to make for a very satisfying cold-weather meal. As usual with these pies, both the filling and crust can be made in advance, then assembled and baked in 30 minutes. The pies are served hot from the oven, but are just as tasty at room temperature.

✺ ✺ ✺

Tip

For a main course, serve an entire pie per person, accompanied by Cucumber Raita and a salad; as an appetizer, slice each pie into quarters and serve on a platter.

PREHEAT OVEN TO 400°F (200°C)
BAKING SHEET, GREASED LIGHTLY WITH VEGETABLE OIL

1	eggplant, unpeeled and cubed (about 1 lb/500 g)	1
1 tsp	salt	5 mL
1/4 cup	vegetable oil	50 mL
2 tbsp	olive oil	25 mL
1/4 tsp	salt	1 mL
1/4 tsp	freshly ground black pepper	1 mL
3 cups	thinly sliced mushrooms	750 mL
4	cloves garlic, thinly sliced	4
1/2 cup	toasted pine nuts	125 mL
1/4 cup	finely chopped fresh mint or 2 tbsp (25 mL) dried	50 mL
1 tbsp	freshly squeezed lemon juice	15 mL
1 tsp	drained capers	5 mL
6	black olives, pitted and roughly chopped	6
4	sheets Olive Oil Crust (see recipe, page 116)	4
1	egg	1
1 tbsp	milk	15 mL
	Cucumber Raita (see recipe, page 167)	

1. Place cubed eggplant and salt in a bowl; add cold water to cover. Mix well and set aside. Let soak for 5 to 10 minutes.

2. In a large frying pan, heat vegetable oil for 1 minute on high heat. Drain eggplant cubes and add to oil. (Careful, the oil will splatter.) Fry for 7 to 8 minutes, stirring and tossing actively, until all the cubes have darkened, softened and are just about to scorch. Transfer to a bowl, along with any pan juices, and set aside.

3. Return pan to the heat. Add olive oil, salt and pepper; stir for 30 seconds. Add mushrooms and stir-fry just until the mushrooms give off liquid, about 2 to 3 minutes. Add garlic and stir-fry for 1 minute. Transfer mixture, along with pan juices, to bowl containing the eggplant. Add pine nuts, mint, lemon juice, capers and olive pieces; fold everything thoroughly to integrate.

4. On a floured surface, lay out sheet of olive oil crust. Spoon one-quarter of the eggplant mixture (about ¾ cup/175 mL) onto the lower half of the crust. Fold the upper half over and, with your fingers or fork, pinch the edges. Place pie on prepared baking sheet. Repeat procedure with the other three pies. Beat the egg and milk together and brush over the crusts. Bake in preheated oven for 20 to 22 minutes, until golden brown and crusty. Serve immediately with Cucumber Raita on the side.

Individual Stuffed Eggplant

SERVES 4 AS A FIRST COURSE OR 2 AS A MAIN COURSE

The original Turkish name for this dish is Imam Bayildi, which means "the imam fainted." The legend goes that an imam, having enjoyed this meal but being of a frugal disposition, asked his wife how much olive oil she had used to make it. When she told him, he fainted in shock. I have reduced the amount of oil for this version, but any way you look at it, this or any other successful eggplant dish is an oil-rich pleasure.

✵ ✵ ✵

PREHEAT OVEN TO 400°F (200°C)
BAKING SHEET, GREASED LIGHTLY WITH VEGETABLE OIL

2	small eggplants (about 2 by 4 inches/5 by 10 cm)	2
1 tsp	salt	5 mL
¼ cup	vegetable oil	50 mL
3 tbsp	olive oil	45 mL
½ tsp	freshly ground black pepper	2 mL
Pinch	ground cinnamon	Pinch
1	onion, finely diced	1
½	green bell pepper, cut into thin strips	½
3	cloves garlic, minced	3
1 tsp	dried oregano leaves	5 mL
2 tbsp	currants or raisins	25 mL
¼ cup	toasted pine nuts	50 mL
1	tomato, sliced	1
	Few sprigs fresh parsley, chopped	

1. Partially slice eggplants lengthwise, without separating them, so they fan open, butterfly-like, skin-side down. Salt the flesh, and let stand for 10 minutes. Rinse them and pat dry.

2. In a large frying pan, heat vegetable oil over high heat until it's just about to smoke. Add eggplants, flesh-side down. (Careful. The oil will splatter, so you may want to use a frying screen.) Reduce heat to medium-high and fry for 2 minutes, until golden brown. Turn (again, carefully: more splatter) and fry the skin side for another 2 minutes. Remove from pan and set on paper towels to drain excess oil.

3. Discard any leftover oil from frying pan. Add olive oil and return to medium-high heat. Add black pepper and cinnamon and stir-fry for 30 seconds. Add onion and cook, stirring, for 2 minutes until the onion wilts. Add green pepper strips and stir-fry for 1 minute. Reduce heat to medium and add minced garlic, oregano and currants. Stir-fry for 2 minutes and remove from heat.

4. Spread fried eggplants, skin-side down on prepared baking sheet. Sprinkle pine nuts evenly over eggplants. Top evenly with fried onion mixture and then tomato slices. (This recipe can now wait for up to 1 hour, uncovered.)

5. Bake in preheated oven for 20 to 25 minutes, until tomatoes have baked down and everything looks shiny. Remove from oven and lift eggplants carefully (to avoid breaking them) onto a serving platter. Garnish with chopped parsley and serve.

Judi's Enchiladas

SERVES 4

This vegetarian Tex-Mex palate-rouser is yet another memento of my long and fondly remembered collaboration with Judi Roe, the superchef of southwestern Quebec. We often used to serve this dish to film crews if it was summer and we could feed them outdoors on picnic tables, instantly igniting a southern ambience.

✳ ✳ ✳

Tips

Corn tortillas are best in this recipe.

Vegans or calorie-conscious types can easily omit both cheese and sour cream, for a leaner but just as delicious meal.

PREHEAT OVEN TO 350°F (180°C)
13-BY 9-INCH (3 L) BAKING DISH, GREASED LIGHTLY WITH VEGETABLE OIL

3 tbsp	vegetable oil	45 mL
1 tbsp	chili powder	15 mL
Pinch	salt	Pinch
1	onion, finely diced	1
2	cloves garlic, minced	2
1 cup	double-strength Vegetable Stock (see recipe and Tips, page 50)	250 mL
1 cup	tomato juice	250 mL
1 tsp	cornstarch	5 mL
1 tbsp	water	15 mL
1	medium tomato, skinned, seeded and finely chopped	1
8 oz	potatoes, boiled and cubed (about 2)	250 g
2 cups	cooked romano beans	500 mL
1½ cups	grated cheese such as Monterey Jack or medium Cheddar	375 mL
12	small tortillas (about 6 inches/15 cm), preferably corn	12
½ cup	sour cream (optional) Few sprigs fresh coriander, chopped	125 mL

1. Make the sauce: In a saucepan, heat vegetable oil over high heat for 30 seconds. Add chili powder and salt and stir for 30 seconds (the oil will turn vibrantly red). Add onion and stir-fry for 2 minutes until softened. Add garlic and stir-fry for 1 minute. Add vegetable stock and tomato juice and bring to boil, stirring. Reduce heat to medium-low and cook, stirring occasionally, for 4 to 5 minutes. Dissolve cornstarch in water; add to sauce, stirring briskly, and cook until the sauce has the consistency of thin syrup. Stir in tomatoes and remove from heat.

2. Make the filling: In a bowl, combine potatoes, beans and grated cheese, folding gently so as to mix thoroughly without mashing potato or beans. Set aside.

3. Assemble the enchiladas: Grasp a tortilla firmly by one edge, dunk in the sauce to coat it, then place in prepared baking dish. Spoon $\frac{1}{3}$ cup (75 mL) of the filling down the center of the tortilla and roll it up like a cigar. Repeat filling procedure with remaining tortillas.

4. Pour remaining sauce evenly over the enchiladas and bake in preheated oven for about 15 minutes, until heated through. Divide enchiladas between 4 dinner plates (3 each) and top with 1 to 2 tbsp (15 to 25 mL) of the sour cream, if using. Garnish with coriander and serve with rice and salad.

Cauliflower Pea Curry

*Kamala McCarthy, who
has already lived enough for
three people, now divides
her time between India and
Quebec's Eastern Townships.
I visited her once on a
perfect July day as she
garnered the daily harvest
from her husband Kabir's
loaded vegetable garden.
We then retired to her sunny
kitchen where she whipped
up this lively vegetable curry
in less than an hour.
Although a relatively simple
concoction, it calls for 18
ingredients — some of
which (black mustard seed,
for example) you may have
to purchase from an East
Indian specialty store.*

❋ ❋ ❋

Tip

Ghee (clarified butter)
can be purchased at East
Indian specialty shops or
made at home by heating
butter over low heat
(without boiling it) and
skimming off whey as it
rises to the surface.

1 1/2 lbs	ripe tomatoes (about 6)	750 g
2	onions, quartered	2
5	cloves garlic, cut in half	5
2 tbsp	minced gingerroot	25 mL
1 tbsp	turmeric	15 mL
1 tbsp	ground coriander	15 mL
2	hot green chilies, chopped	2
1/4 cup	ghee (clarified butter) (see Tip, left)	50 mL
1 tsp	black mustard seeds	5 mL
1 tsp	whole cumin seeds	5 mL
1 tsp	whole fennel seeds	5 mL
1 tbsp	salt	15 mL
1	head cauliflower, florets only	1
3/4 cup	frozen peas	175 mL
1 tbsp	chopped fresh mint	15 mL
1 tsp	garam masala	5 mL
1/2 cup	yogurt	125 mL
2 tbsp	chopped fresh coriander	25 mL
	Mango Raita (see recipe, page 168)	
	Spinach Dal (see recipe, page 132)	
	Steamed rice	

1. Blanch tomatoes in boiling water for 30 seconds.
   Over a bowl, peel, core and deseed them. Chop
   tomatoes into chunks and set aside. Strain any
   accumulated tomato juices from bowl; add the
   juices to the tomatoes.

2. In a food processor, add onions, garlic, ginger,
   turmeric, coriander and chilies; process at high until
   thoroughly minced. Transfer mixture to a bowl.

Individual Vegetable Goat Cheese Pie (page 118)
with Olive Oil Crust (page 116)

Overleaf (clockwise from upper left): Cauliflower Pea Curry (this page),
Spinach Dal (page 132) and Mango Raita (page 168)

3. Put tomatoes and tomato juices into the same food processor (you needn't bother washing it) and purée.

4. In a large saucepan, heat clarified butter over medium heat for 1 minute. Add mustard, cumin and fennel seeds; stir-fry 2 to 3 minutes until the various seeds begin to pop. Add reserved onion-garlic mixture and stir-fry until it all begins to darken, about 4 to 5 minutes. Add tomato purée and cook, stirring, for 5 minutes.

5. Stir salt and cauliflower into the sauce. Cook, uncovered, for 20 minutes, stirring occasionally.

6. Add frozen peas, mint and garam masala; fold together gently and cook for 3 to 4 minutes. Fold in yogurt and cook for 1 to 2 minutes; fold again and remove from heat. Let curry rest for a few minutes, uncovered. Transfer to a serving bowl and garnish generously with coriander. Serve with Mango Raita, Spinach Dal and steamed rice.

Chickpea Tofu Stew (page 131)

Individual Broccoli Ricotta Pie

SERVES 4

As part of my ongoing quest to make the very healthy broccoli palatable (even desirable), I offer this simple but flavorful pie, suitable both for everyday and for festive dining. It offers pleasant textures and an amalgam of individual tastes that blend refreshingly together. It's low in calories and a snap to make. It kinda has it all.

✸ ✸ ✸

PREHEAT OVEN TO 400°F (200°C)
4 RAMEKINS, 1½ CUP (375 mL) CAPACITY, MEASURING 1 TO 2 INCHES (2.5 TO 5 CM) DEEP AND 5 INCHES (12.5 CM) WIDE

3 cups	broccoli florets	750 mL
1 tbsp	freshly squeezed lemon juice	15 mL
¼ tsp	salt	1 mL
¼ tsp	freshly ground black pepper	1 mL
2 tbsp	olive oil	25 mL
½ cup	thinly sliced red onion	125 mL
1	red bell pepper, cut into strips	1
¼ cup	chopped fresh dill	50 mL
1	medium tomato, sliced	1
1 cup	fresh ricotta cheese	250 mL
4	sheets Olive Oil Crust (see recipe, page 116)	4
1	egg	1
1 tbsp	milk	15 mL
3 tbsp	Aïoli (see recipe, page 162)	45 mL
1 cup	yogurt	250 mL

1. In a large saucepan, boil broccoli florets for 4 to 5 minutes. Drain, rinse under cold water and drain again. Transfer broccoli to a bowl and stir in lemon juice, salt and pepper.

2. In a large frying pan, heat oil over high heat for 30 seconds. Add onions and peppers and stir-fry for 4 to 5 minutes until softened and just starting to char.

3. Divide broccoli evenly among ramekins, covering the bottom of each. Create a second layer in each ramekin with the onion-pepper mixture, then sprinkle with dill. Create another layer with the sliced tomatoes, then top with a quarter of the ricotta. Press down the ricotta to spread it out slightly.

4. Cover the filling with a sheet of crust, pinching the excess pastry to the outside edges of rims. Whisk together the egg and milk and brush over the crusts. Bake in preheated oven for 20 to 22 minutes, until golden brown and crusty. Mix Aïoli and yogurt together and transfer to a serving bowl. Serve pies immediately with this sauce on the side.

Chickpea Tofu Stew

VEGAN RECIPE

SERVES 4

A filling and flavorful winter dish, this stew is bolstered with the addition of the super-nutritious tofu. It is imperative to use firm tofu (often called "pressed tofu"), since the soft variety will disintegrate. For chickpeas, you can either cook your own, or use the canned variety.

Tips

Excellent served with a salad, steamed rice and a yogurt-based sauce.

For a spicier flavor, substitute cayenne pepper for the chili powder.

PREHEAT OVEN TO 375°F (190°C)
6-CUP (1.5 L) CASSEROLE DISH

1 lb	ripe tomatoes (about 4)	500 g
3 tbsp	olive oil	45 mL
1/2 tsp	salt	2 mL
1/2 tsp	paprika	2 mL
1/2 tsp	cumin seeds	2 mL
1/2 tsp	chili powder	2 mL
2 1/2 cups	thinly sliced onion	625 mL
1/2	green pepper, thinly sliced	1/2
4	cloves garlic, thinly sliced	4
2	bay leaves	2
1 cup	hot water	250 mL
2 tsp	lime juice	10 mL
2 cups	cooked chickpeas	500 mL
8 oz	firm tofu, cut into 1/2-inch (1 cm) cubes	250 g
1 tsp	olive oil (optional)	5 mL
1/4 cup	finely diced red onion	50 mL
	Few sprigs fresh coriander, chopped	

1. Blanch tomatoes in boiling water for 30 seconds. Over a bowl, peel, core and deseed them. Chop tomatoes into chunks and set aside. Strain any accumulated tomato juices from bowl; add the juices to the tomatoes.
2. In a large frying pan, heat olive oil over high heat for 30 seconds. Add salt, paprika, cumin seeds and chili powder in quick succession. Stir-fry for 30 seconds. Add onions and stir-fry for 1 minute. Add green peppers and stir-fry for 2 to 3 minutes until soft. Add garlic and stir-fry for 1 minute. Add tomato flesh and juices. Stir-cook for 3 minutes to break up tomato somewhat. Add bay leaves, hot water and lime juice. Cook, stirring often, for 5 minutes.
3. Transfer sauce to casserole dish. Fold chickpeas into the sauce. Distribute tofu cubes evenly over the surface, and gently press them down into the sauce.
4. Bake in preheated oven, uncovered, for 25 to 30 minutes, until bubbling and bright. Drizzle with olive oil, if using, and garnish with red onions and coriander.

Spinach Dal

SERVES 6

This flavorful, soothing and very nutritious Indian lentil (dal) recipe shows the flip-side of chef Kamala McCarthy's spicy cooking. She serves it over rice with a vegetable curry (like her Cauliflower Pea Curry) for a balanced meal. Kamala prefers to use chana dal, which requires one hour of soaking and 1 1/2 hours of cooking. Instead, I've chosen masoor dal, the tiny red lentil that needs next to no soaking and cooks quickly. Admittedly, I lose the nuttier texture of the chana, but I gain the creamy, rich consistency of the smaller lentil, as well as its vibrant color.

※ ※ ※

Tip

Ghee (clarified butter) can be purchased at East Indian specialty shops or made at home by heating butter over low heat (without boiling it) and skimming off whey as it rises to the surface.

3 1/2 cups	masoor dal (red lentils), rinsed and drained	875 mL
8 cups	water	2 L
1 tbsp	turmeric	15 mL
1 tsp	whole cloves	5 mL
3	bay leaves	3
2 tbsp	ghee (clarified butter) (see Tip, left)	25 mL
2	onions, finely chopped	2
2 tbsp	minced gingerroot	25 mL
5	cloves garlic, minced	5
6 cups	chopped fresh spinach, packed down	1.5 L
1 tbsp	salt	15 mL
1/4 cup	ghee (clarified butter)	50 mL
1 tsp	black mustard seeds	5 mL
1 tsp	whole cumin seeds	5 mL
4 tsp	garam masala	20 mL
2 tbsp	chopped fresh coriander	25 mL
	Cucumber Raita (see recipe, page 167)	
	Cauliflower Pea Curry (see recipe, page 128)	
	Steamed rice	

1. Put dal and water into a large pot and bring to a boil. Remove from heat. Add turmeric, cloves and bay leaves and stir. Let sit for 10 to 15 minutes until dal has swollen and has soaked up much of the water.

2. Place the lentil pot over high heat and cook for 5 to 7 minutes, stirring occasionally, until bubbling. Reduce heat to medium and cook for another 15 to 20 minutes, stirring occasionally, until the dal is tender. (If the dal dries out, add 1 or 2 cups boiling water.)

3. Meanwhile, in a frying pan, heat 2 tbsp (25 mL) ghee over high heat for 30 seconds. Add onions and stir-fry for 2 minutes. Add ginger and garlic, and stir-fry for another 2 minutes. Remove from heat and add to the dal. Continue cooking the dal with its new additions for 5 minutes, stirring occasionally. Add spinach strips and salt, stir well and cook for 10 minutes.

4. Meanwhile, in a small saucepan, heat $1/4$ cup (50 mL) ghee over medium heat for 1 minute. Add mustard and cumin seeds. Stir-fry for 2 to 3 minutes until the seeds begin to pop. Add this mixture to the simmering dal. The hot fat will hit the wet lentils with a distinct sizzle (this is called a "chaunk"). Stir, and add 3 tsp (45 mL) of the garam masala. Stir again, reduce heat to medium-low, and cook for 5 minutes, stirring occasionally.

5. Remove from heat and let rest, uncovered, for 15 minutes. Transfer to a serving bowl, sprinkle with the remaining garam masala and the coriander. Serve accompanied by Cucumber Raita, Cauliflower Pea Curry and steamed rice.

Vegetarian Moussaka Pie

SERVES 15 TO 20

The Greeks borrowed the Eastern idea of combining fried eggplant with a meat sauce and turned it into a glorious cheese-crusted centerpiece party dish. I've eliminated the meat and increased the aromatic vegetable content to create this highly satisfying alternative. I offer a large buffet-size version because the multi-step recipe is not worth it for smaller quantities. At this size, you'll spend as long on it as you would for any other dish providing an equivalent number of portions.

✳ ✳ ✳

PREHEAT OVEN TO 350°F (180°C)
16-BY 12-INCH (40 BY 30 CM) DEEP BAKING DISH

Eggplant Layer

3	eggplants (each about 1 lb/500 g)	3
1 tbsp	salt	15 mL
1 cup	vegetable oil, divided	250 mL

Potato Layer

3 lbs	potatoes, unpeeled and scrubbed, thickly sliced (about 9 potatoes)	1.5 kg
1/2 cup	vegetable oil	125 mL

Vegetable Sauce Layer

1	bunch broccoli	1
1/4 cup	olive oil	50 mL
2 tsp	salt	10 mL
1 tsp	freshly ground black pepper	5 mL
2 cups	thinly sliced onion	500 mL
1	green bell pepper, thinly sliced	1
1	red bell pepper, thinly sliced	1
3 cups	sliced mushrooms	750 mL
4 cups	Tomato Sauce (see recipe, page 138)	1 L
1 tsp	dried oregano leaves	5 mL
2 cups	ricotta cheese	500 mL

Cheese Topping

4 cups	milk	1 L
2	bay leaves	2
1/2 cup	butter	125 mL
1/2 tsp	grated nutmeg	2 mL
1/2 tsp	salt	2 mL
1/2 tsp	freshly ground black pepper	2 mL
2/3 cup	all-purpose flour	150 mL
2 cups	shredded mozzarella	500 mL
1/4 cup	finely grated Romano cheese	50 mL
6	eggs, well beaten	6

1. Prepare eggplant: Cut stems off eggplants. Peel a 2-inch (5 cm) belt of skin lengthwise down one side of each eggplant and up the other. Standing eggplant upright on stem end, and starting with a skinned side, slice each eggplant vertically into 4 slices. Each slice will have a border of skin. Sprinkle salt on both sides of all the slices and set aside.

2. Make potato layer: In a large frying pan, heat ½ cup (125 mL) vegetable oil on medium-high heat for 1 minute. In 3 batches, fry potato slices 2 to 3 minutes on each side until golden brown but not necessarily cooked through. Transfer each batch as it's fried to the baking dish, arranging the potatoes in a single layer covering the bottom of the dish. Discard excess oil.

3. Make the vegetable sauce: Cut off bottom half of broccoli stalks and reserve for another use. Separate the rest into branches and boil on high heat for 4 minutes. Drain, refresh with iced water, drain again, and chop finely. Set aside.

4. Heat ¼ cup (50 mL) olive oil in a large frying pan over high heat. Add salt and pepper and stir. Add onions, green and red peppers, and stir-fry for 4 to 5 minutes until well wilted. Add sliced mushrooms and fold in, stir-frying for 3 to 4 minutes, until everything appears moist and shiny. Transfer vegetable mixture to a bowl. Add tomato sauce, oregano and chopped broccoli; mix well. Spread the vegetable mixture over potatoes in baking dish, then add ricotta in generous but evenly spaced dollops on top.

5. Fry eggplant: In a large frying pan, heat ½ cup (125 mL) of the vegetable oil over medium-high heat. Quickly rinse and drain the salted eggplant slices. Fry the slices in batches, 2 to 3 minutes per side until brown. Add more oil for subsequent batches as necessary. As a batch of eggplant is ready, transfer it to a paper towel to drain, and then form a single layer of eggplant on top of the ricotta in the pan. With the eggplant layer in place, this recipe can now wait to be completed at leisure.

continued on next page...

6. Make the cheese topping: In a small saucepan, heat milk with bay leaves over low heat until hot but not scalding. Meanwhile, in a deep saucepan, stir-melt butter with nutmeg, salt and pepper over medium heat until bubbling but not browning, about 3 to 4 minutes. Add flour and stir actively for 3 to 4 minutes, until all the flour is absorbed and the mixture, or roux, has returned to a bubble, sticking slightly to the pan.

7. Remove bay leaves from hot milk and add milk all at once to the roux, whisking until it starts to thicken. Reduce heat to medium-low and cook, stirring, for 3 to 4 minutes, until the sauce is like heavy cream. Remove from heat and let cool for 5 to 6 minutes.

8. Add mozzarella and Romano cheeses to the sauce and whisk to mix well. Add the beaten eggs in a steady stream, whisking actively, until homogenized. Spread sauce over the eggplant layer in the pan to cover the whole surface evenly.

9. Bake in preheated oven for 1 hour until the top is firm to the touch and browned nicely along the edges. Remove from oven and cut the moussaka into 20 slices (4 cuts vertically and 5 horizontally). Do not try to unmold; serve in the baking pan on the buffet or table, lifting portions off the pan directly onto plates.

Pasta, Polenta & Rice

Tomato Sauce

VEGAN RECIPE

MAKES 4 CUPS (1 L), ENOUGH FOR PASTA SERVING 8

Two thousand years after the fall of the Roman Empire, the residents of the Italian peninsula have found a way to conquer the planet: through their pasta cookery. Possibly the most famous of all pastas (and indeed, a synonym for the very concept) is spaghetti with tomato sauce. My list of pasta recipes therefore begins with this quick-to-make tomato sauce for spaghetti. This is a generic tomato-basil-garlic sauce that works not only with spaghetti, but with whatever recipe calls for a tomato enhancement. It freezes well, and is easy to make in large batches. It is very useful to have on hand.

Tip

Canned, whole plum tomatoes can replace fresh. Use 2 cans (each 28 oz/796 mL), reserving 2 cups (500 mL) of the juice for use if the sauce needs thinning.

3 lbs	ripe tomatoes (see Tip, left)	1.5 kg
1/3 cup	olive oil	75 mL
Pinch	salt	Pinch
8	cloves garlic, roughly chopped	8
1/2 tsp	hot pepper flakes	2 mL
1 1/2 tbsp	dried basil or 1/4 to 1/2 cup (50 to 125 mL) chopped fresh basil, packed down	20 mL
1 tbsp	balsamic vinegar	15 mL
6	sun-dried tomatoes, finely chopped	6

1. Blanch tomatoes in boiling water for 30 seconds. Over a bowl, peel, core and deseed them. Chop tomatoes roughly and set aside. Strain any accumulated tomato juices from bowl; add half of the juices to the chopped tomatoes. Save or freeze the other half for recipes that call for tomato juice.
2. In a large, deep frying pan or pot, heat oil over high heat for 30 seconds. Add salt and stir. Add chopped garlic and stir-fry for 30 seconds. Add the hot pepper flakes and stir-fry for 30 seconds.
3. Add chopped tomatoes and juices. Stir-cook until boiling. Add basil (if using dried), the vinegar and sun-dried tomatoes. Mix well, and reduce heat to medium-low. Cook for 20 to 25 minutes, maintaining a steady bubbling, stirring occasionally.
4. If using fresh basil, add it now to taste (no amount is too much). Stir in, and continue cooking for 5 minutes. Remove from heat and cover. Let rest for 5 to 10 minutes to develop flavor. Stir to redistribute the oil that has risen to the top, and serve immediately.

Spaghettini with Capers

**SERVES 4 AS A PASTA
COURSE OR 2 AS
A MAIN COURSE**

*A sparely sauced pasta,
it combines the basic
ingredients of pesto
(basil, pine nuts, garlic)
with the tartness of capers
on the long, thin noodles.
It works beautifully as a
pasta course or as the main
course of a light dinner.
Fresh basil is a must here.*

❋ ❋ ❋

8 oz	spaghettini	250 g
1/4 cup	olive oil	50 mL
3	cloves garlic, lightly crushed but not pressed	3
2	dried red chilies	2
1/2 tsp	salt	2 mL
1/4 cup	chopped fresh basil, packed down	50 mL
2 tbsp	toasted pine nuts	25 mL
2 tbsp	drained capers	25 mL
	Grated Romano cheese (optional)	

1. In a large pot of boiling water, cook pasta according to package directions until tender but firm.

2. Meanwhile, in a deep frying pan, heat olive oil over medium-high heat for 30 seconds. Add garlic and chilies. Stir occasionally, cooking until garlic and chilies have started to turn dark brown, about 3 or 4 minutes. Remove from heat; pick out garlic and chilies and discard.

3. Place pan back on heat. Add salt and basil; stir-fry for 30 seconds until basil has wilted. Remove from heat and add pine nuts and capers. Mix well and set aside.

4. Drain pasta and transfer it to the frying pan. Toss well, making sure sauce is well distributed. Serve immediately with grated cheese, if using, on the side.

Linguine Barolo

SERVES 4 AS A PASTA COURSE OR 2 AS A MAIN COURSE

This palate-dazzler comes from Margie and Michael Pagliaro restauranteurs. Simple and relatively inexpensive (considering its elegance) it's ideal for parties, since the linguine can be cooked in advance and the sauce prepared at the last moment.

❈ ❈ ❈

8 oz	linguine	250 g
2 tbsp	olive oil	25 mL
¾ cup	half-and-half (10%) cream or half 10% cream and half double-strength Vegetable Broth (see recipe and Tips, page 50)	175 mL
2 oz	Gorgonzola cheese, crumbled	60 g
4	sun-dried tomatoes, cut into ½-inch (1 cm) strips	4
1½ cups	broccoli florets	375 mL
¼ cup	toasted pine nuts	50 mL
	Few sprigs fresh parsley, chopped	

1. In a large pot of boiling salted water, cook pasta according to package directions until tender but firm. Drain pasta and add olive oil; toss until well coated. Cover and set aside.

2. In a skillet, heat cream (or cream-broth mixture, if using) over medium heat until it begins to steam. Add Gorgonzola and stir until cheese has dissolved (about 2 minutes). Reduce heat to medium-low and add sun-dried tomatoes and broccoli; continue cooking, stirring occasionally, until the sauce is smooth and the broccoli tender, about 4 to 5 minutes.

3. Increase heat to medium. Add linguine. Toss and cook for 2 to 3 minutes, until pasta is well coated and heated through. Serve garnished with pine nuts and parsley.

Fusilli with Leeks

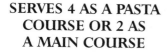

*Take colorful, ridged fusilli
and a smooth, pink sauce
studded with green-and-
white leeks. What have you
got? A surefire crowd pleaser
— irresistible, even for the
most fickle of appetites.
Fat-conscious types may
shudder at the use of 35%
cream, but the quantity is
modest and the taste
benefits are immense. If
you must, use 10% cream
instead. You can even
omit the cream entirely,
but at significant loss of
smoothness and richness.*

❋ ❋ ❋

Tip

Be sure to wash leek
thoroughly, splitting
down the middle and
paying special care to
the grit that hides where
the green and white
parts meet.

2	tomatoes	2
3 cups	3-color fusilli	750 mL
3 tbsp	olive oil, divided	40 mL
¼ tsp	salt	1 mL
¼ tsp	freshly ground black pepper	1 mL
2 cups	finely chopped leek, green and white parts alike (see Tip, left)	500 mL
Pinch	dried oregano leaves	Pinch
1 tsp	chopped fresh sage or a pinch dried	5 mL
½ cup	double-strength Vegetable Stock (see recipe and Tips, page 50)	125 mL
2 tbsp	whipping (35%) cream or 3 tbsp (45 mL) half-and-half (10%) cream	25 mL
	Grated Romano cheese	

1. Blanch tomatoes in boiling water for 30 seconds. Over a bowl, peel, core and deseed them. Chop tomatoes roughly and set aside. Strain any accumulated tomato juices from bowl; add to the chopped tomatoes.

2. In a large pot of boiling salted water, cook pasta according to package directions until tender but firm. Rinse pasta and drain. Add 1 tbsp (15 mL) olive oil and toss; cover and set aside.

3. Meanwhile, in a large frying pan, heat 2 tbsp (25 mL) oil over high heat for 30 seconds. Add salt and pepper and stir. Add chopped leeks and stir-fry until softened, about 2 to 3 minutes. Add oregano and sage and stir-fry for 30 seconds.

4. Stir in tomatoes and juice, mashing down the tomato. Add broth and bring to a boil, continuing to mash tomatoes and stirring for 2 to 3 minutes. Reduce heat to minimum; add cream, stirring to mix evenly, and cook for 2 to 3 minutes. Toss pasta with sauce; transfer to serving bowls. Top with grated cheese and serve immediately.

Fettuccine with Fennel and Artichokes

SERVES 4

Here is a sparely sauced pasta that is quick to make but as elegant as a more belabored creation. The only tricky bit is the final assembly and integration into the sauce, which must be handled carefully (it can be messy) and efficiently so that each portion gets its share of the treats.

✳ ✳ ✳

Tip

The fennel bulb always comes attached to woody branches and thin leaves that look like dill. Cut off and discard the woody branches and thin leaves. Quarter the bulb vertically, then cut out and discard the hard triangular sections of core. What remains is the usable part of the fennel.

¼ cup	olive oil	50 mL
½ tsp	salt	2 mL
¼ tsp	freshly ground black pepper	1 mL
½ tsp	fennel seeds	2 mL
1	fennel bulb, trimmed, cored and cut into ½ inch (1 cm) pieces (about 2 cups/500 mL) (see Tip, left)	1
1	medium tomato, cut into ½-inch (1 cm) wedges	1
4	sun-dried tomatoes, thinly sliced	4
1 tsp	balsamic vinegar	5 mL
1 tsp	dried basil leaves	5 mL
1	jar (6 oz/175 mL) marinated artichoke hearts, drained	1
¼ cup	white wine	50 mL
1 lb	fettuccine	500 g
	Shredded sharp Italian cheese such as Pecorino, Crotonese, aged Provolone or Romano (optional) Several sprigs fresh basil and/or parsley, chopped	

1. In a large deep frying pan, heat olive oil, salt, pepper and fennel seeds for 1 minute over high heat. Add fresh fennel pieces; sauté for 3 minutes or until the fennel is beginning to color. Add tomato wedges, sun-dried tomatoes, vinegar and dried basil; cook, stirring, for 2 to 3 minutes or until tomatoes have broken down and a sauce is forming. Add artichokes and wine, reduce heat to medium and cook, stirring, for 2 minutes or until the sauce is bubbling again. Take off heat and reserve in frying pan.

2. In a large pot of boiling salted water, cook the fettuccine until tender but firm; drain.

3. Return frying pan to medium heat. Add the fettuccine. Toss and combine for 1 to 2 minutes or until all the pasta is coated with the sauce. Serve immediately, garnished with cheese, if using, and herbs.

Penne with Eggplant and Mushrooms

SERVES 4

This pasta dish has a messy, peasant look and feel to it, making it ideal for a casual get-together. The sweetness of the boiled-then-sautéed eggplant melts into the sauce, giving the dish its "informal" look, while providing a feast for the taste buds. The assembly of sauce with pasta in Step 4 requires care and patience to ensure thorough integration.

❋ ❋ ❋

2 cups	cubed peeled eggplant	500 mL
1/4 cup	olive oil	50 mL
1/2 tsp	salt	2 mL
1/4 tsp	freshly ground black pepper	1 mL
6 oz	wild or button mushrooms, trimmed and halved	175 g
4	cloves garlic, thinly sliced	4
1	medium tomato, cut into 1/2-inch (1 cm) wedges	1
1 tsp	dried basil leaves	5 mL
1/2 tsp	balsamic vinegar	2 mL
1/4 cup	water	50 mL
12 oz	penne noodles	375 g
	Few sprigs fresh basil and/or parsley, chopped	

1. Bring a pot of salted water to the boil while peeling and cutting eggplant. (Keep in mind that eggplant doesn't like to wait long after it's cut and will quickly turn brown.) Add eggplant to the boiling water, reduce heat to medium and cook 5 to 6 minutes or until eggplant is tender and softened. Drain and set aside.

2. In a large deep frying pan, heat olive oil, salt and pepper over high heat for 1 minute. Add mushrooms and eggplant; stir-fry for 3 minutes or until mushrooms are softened and eggplant begins to break up. Add garlic and stir-fry for 30 seconds. Add tomato, basil and vinegar; cook, stirring, for 2 to 3 minutes or until the tomato has broken down and a sauce is forming. Add water, reduce heat to medium and cook, stirring, for 1 minute or until the sauce is bubbling again. Take off heat and reserve in frying pan.

3. In a large pot of boiling salted water, cook penne until tender but firm; drain.

4. Return frying pan to medium heat. Add penne. Toss and combine for 1 to 2 minutes or until all the pasta is coated with the sauce. Serve immediately, garnished with herbs.

Pasta with Coriander Pesto and Peppers

SERVES 4

An alternative to basil pesto, this is a welcome accompaniment to pasta dishes. It is very easy to concoct and is certain to impress even those who believe they have eaten enough pesto for a lifetime.

❋ ❋ ❋

Pesto

1 cup	packed roughly chopped coriander	250 mL
1/2 cup	grated strong Italian cheese such as Asiago, Crotonese or aged Provolone (about 2 oz/60 g)	125 mL
1/4 cup	pine nuts	50 mL
2 tbsp	lime juice	25 mL
1 to 2 tbsp	minced fresh hot chilies or 1/4 to 1/2 tsp (1 to 2 mL) cayenne pepper	15 to 25 mL
1/4 tsp	salt	1 mL
1/8 tsp	freshly ground black pepper	0.5 mL
1/4 cup	extra virgin olive oil	50 mL
1 tbsp	olive oil	15 mL
1/2	green bell pepper, cut into 1/4-inch (0.5 cm) strips	1/2
1/2	red bell pepper, cut into 1/4-inch (0.5 cm) strips	1/2
12 oz	short pasta (such as penne or fusilli) Extra virgin olive oil for sprinkling	375 g

1. Make the pesto: In a food processor, combine coriander, cheese, pine nuts, lime juice, chilies, salt and pepper; process until finely chopped. With machine running, add 1/4 cup (50 mL) olive oil through the feed tube; continue to process until smooth, scraping down sides of bowl once. You should have about 1 cup (250 mL) of a bright green, dense paste. Divide in half. Store one half for another use, tightly covered, in refrigerator for up to 3 days. Set other half aside.

2. In a frying pan, heat 1 tbsp (15 mL) olive oil over medium-high heat. Cook pepper strips for 5 minutes or until softened and a little bit charred. Set aside in frying pan.

3. In a large pot of boiling salted water, cook the pasta until tender but firm; drain. Transfer pasta to a warm bowl; add ½ cup (125 mL) of the pesto. Stir and toss actively to distribute the pesto evenly. Add the reserved peppers with the pan juices and toss to combine.

4. Serve immediately, with extra virgin olive oil on the side.

Mushroom-Spinach Lasagna with Goat Cheese

SERVES 4 TO 6

Lasagna layered with meat, cheese and tomato sauce is so much a part of our gastronomic vocabulary that contemplating one with different ingredients requires a considerable stretch of the imagination. Still, there's a world of lasagnas out there. So if you're in the mood for a change, try this meatless variety — it's every bit as satisfying as the original.

❈ ❈ ❈

Tips

If expense or calories are a concern, you can substitute low-fat ricotta for the goat cheese in the filling, as well as 12 oz (375 g) low-fat mozzarella instead of the recommended mixture for the topping.

For noodles, either cook your own or use the "ready to bake" variety (preferably white ones, to contrast with the spinach).

PREHEAT OVEN TO 375°F (190°C)
13-BY 9-INCH (3 L) BAKING DISH

12 oz	spinach, washed and trimmed	375 g
¼ cup	olive oil, divided	50 mL
¾ tsp	salt, divided	4 mL
½ tsp	freshly ground black pepper, divided	2 mL
12 oz	portobello mushrooms, trimmed and sliced ½-inch (1 cm) thick	375 g
2 tbsp	finely chopped garlic, divided	25 mL
½ tsp	hot pepper flakes	2 mL
2 cups	finely diced peeled tomatoes, with juices or canned tomatoes	500 mL
1 tsp	balsamic vinegar	5 mL
½ tsp	dried rosemary, crumbled	2 mL
½ tsp	dried thyme leaves	2 mL
9	cooked lasagna noodles (see Tips, left)	9
8 oz	goat cheese, divided (see Tips, left)	250 g
8 oz	shredded mozzarella (about 2 cups/500 mL)	250 g
4 oz	grated strong Italian cheese such as Crotonese, Asiago or aged Provolone	125 g

1. In a large pot, bring about 1 inch (2.5 cm) salted water to boil. Add spinach, cover and cook for 1 minute. Uncover, turn the spinach, cover again and cook 1 minute more. Drain. Rinse under cold water; drain. Press lightly to extract more water and set aside in a colander to continue draining.

2. In a large nonstick frying pan, heat 2 tbsp (25 mL) of the olive oil, ¼ tsp (0.5 mL) of the salt and ¼ tsp (0.5 mL) of the pepper over high heat for 1 minute. Add mushroom slices (they'll absorb all the oil immediately); stir-fry for 3 to 4 minutes or until browned and shiny. Add 1 tbsp (15 mL) of the garlic and stir-fry for 1 minute or until the garlic starts to brown. Transfer to a bowl and set aside.

3. In the same frying pan, heat remaining olive oil, remaining salt, remaining pepper, hot pepper flakes and remaining garlic over high heat, stirring, for 1 minute. Add tomatoes, vinegar, rosemary and thyme; cook, stirring, until bubbling. Cook, stirring, for 2 more minutes or until the tomatoes are breaking up and a sauce forms. Remove from heat and set aside.

4. Spread the bottom of baking dish with 2 tbsp (25 mL) of the tomato sauce. Lay flat 3 of the lasagna noodles (they should cover the whole surface). Spread the spinach evenly over the surface. Dot half of the goat cheese evenly over the spinach. Cover with another layer of 3 noodles. Spread the mushrooms evenly over lasagna noodles. Dot remaining goat cheese over the mushrooms. Cover with the last layer of 3 noodles and spoon the rest of the tomato sauce evenly over the noodles. Mix the grated mozzarella and strong Italian cheeses; sprinkle evenly over the surface of the lasagna to create the topping.

5. Bake in preheated oven, uncovered, for 35 to 40 minutes or until the topping is rosy-browned and the inside is bubbling. Remove from oven and let rest, uncovered, for 10 minutes to temper. Lift portions carefully to retain the cheese on top and serve immediately.

Baked Orzo and Beans

SERVES 4 TO 6

Orzo — a jumbo rice lookalike — may be the most versatile of all pastas. This recipe comes from a long line of similarly baked Greek dishes, but borrows from Italian cuisine in its cheese topping. Use a plainer tomato sauce (mine may be too piquant) and omit the sautéed red onion, and you'll have a dish that delights young children, who seem to have a natural affinity to orzo (maybe because it's so much fun to pick up individual grains with tiny fingers).

❋ ❋ ❋

Preheat oven to 350°F (180°C)
10-cup (2.5 L) casserole with lid

2½ cups	orzo	625 mL
1 tbsp	olive oil	15 mL
½ cup	sliced red onion	125 mL
2	tomatoes, roughly chopped	2
2 cups	Tomato Sauce (see recipe, page 50)	500 mL
2 cups	cooked red kidney beans	500 mL
1 cup	tomato juice	250 mL
1 cup	shaved Parmesan cheese	250 mL
1 tbsp	extra virgin olive oil	15 mL
	Few sprigs fresh parsley, chopped	
	Grated Romano cheese (optional)	

1. In a large pot of boiling salted water, cook orzo until al dente, about 10 minutes.

2. Meanwhile, in a skillet, heat oil over high heat for 30 seconds; add onions and cook, stirring, for 1 or 2 minutes, until slightly charred. Remove from heat and set aside.

3. When orzo is cooked, drain well and transfer to casserole. Add sautéed onions to orzo and stir to combine. Add tomatoes and tomato sauce; mix thoroughly. Add cooked beans; fold until evenly distributed.

4. Cover orzo mixture and bake in preheated oven, covered, for 30 minutes. Remove from oven and mix in tomato juice. Top with Parmesan shavings and return to the oven, uncovered, for another 10 to 12 minutes, until the cheese is melted. Serve on pasta plates, making sure each portion is topped with some of the melted cheese. Drizzle a few drops of extra virgin olive oil on each portion and garnish with chopped parsley. Serve immediately, with Romano, if using, as an accompaniment.

Mumaliga (Romanian Polenta)

SERVES 4

Margaret Dragu, with whom I've enjoyed a long post-modern marriage, swears by the comforts of this ultra-simple dish, which was a staple of her Romanian home on the Canadian Prairies. I like it because it is light yet filling, and infinitely adaptable: it goes with just about anything you wish to serve with it.

2½ cups	water	625 mL
½ tsp	salt	2 mL
1 cup	yellow cornmeal	250 mL
1 cup	cottage cheese	250 mL
½ cup	sour cream	125 mL
4	green onions, finely chopped	4
	Freshly ground black pepper to taste	

1. In a large saucepan, bring water to a rolling boil over high heat. Add salt. Add cornmeal in a thin but steady stream, stirring constantly (preferably with a wooden spoon). Reduce heat to medium-low, and continue stirring for 2 to 3 minutes, until the mixture is smooth and has thickened to the consistency of mashed potatoes.

2. Transfer the mumaliga to a medium bowl and cover with an inverted plate. Let set for about 5 minutes.

3. Holding the bowl and plate together, turn the mumaliga onto the plate. (A small tap on the bottom of the bowl will help it to dislodge it from the bowl.) It will be soft but dense, holding the shape of a small cake.

4. Quarter the cake, and cut each quarter into 3 slices. They'll be sticky but separable. Place 3 slices on each of 4 plates. Top each portion with ¼ cup (50 mL) of the cottage cheese and 2 tbsp (25 mL) of the sour cream. Garnish with green onions and black pepper; serve immediately.

Polenta with Fried Tomato

SERVES 4

My father, Apostol, was sent to private school in Bucharest, Romania in the 1930s — when it was the Paris of Eastern Europe — where he developed a passion for mumaliga (see recipe, page 149), whether served fresh or refried the next day as leftovers. This dish, with its Italian overtones, was originally intended for leftover mumaliga. But I prefer to make a fresh batch of mumaliga (or polenta).

✳ ✳ ✳

2½ cups	water	625 mL
½ tsp	salt	2 mL
1 cup	yellow cornmeal	250 mL
¼ cup	olive oil	50 mL
2 tbsp	butter	25 mL
¼ tsp	salt	1 mL
¼ tsp	freshly ground black pepper	1 mL
½ cup	sliced red onion	125 mL
½	green bell pepper, cut into strips	½
2	ripe medium tomatoes, cut into eighths	2
3	cloves garlic, thinly sliced	3
1 tsp	dried basil leaves	5 mL
4 oz	soft goat cheese, crumbled	125 g
	Few sprigs fresh basil and/or parsley, chopped	
4	black olives, pitted and chopped	4

1. In a large saucepan, bring water to a rolling boil over high heat. Add salt. Add cornmeal in a thin but steady stream, stirring constantly (preferably with a wooden spoon). Reduce heat to medium-low, and continue stirring for 2 to 3 minutes, until the mixture is smooth and has thickened to the consistency of mashed potatoes.

2. Transfer the mumaliga to a medium bowl and cover with an inverted plate. Let set for about 5 minutes.

3. Holding the bowl and plate together, turn the mumaliga onto the plate. (A small tap on the bottom of the bowl will help it to dislodge it from the bowl.) It will be soft but dense, holding the shape of a small cake. Quarter the cake, and cut each quarter into 3 slices.

4. In a large frying pan, heat oil and butter over medium-high heat for 1 minute. Stir in salt and pepper. Add red onions and green peppers to pan in a single layer. Make another layer of polenta wedges and cook for 4 minutes, until starting to scorch. Flip the polenta over (the onions and peppers will turn over, too). Reduce heat to medium and fry this side for 4 minutes.

5. Flip polenta again and fry the first side for another 2 minutes until all the ingredients are slightly browned. Push polenta and vegetables to the sides of the pan. Increase heat to medium-high and add the tomato wedges to the vacated center of the pan; fry for 2 to 3 minutes until tomatoes begin to soften. Sprinkle garlic and basil over everything and then gently fold the tomatoes and polenta together for 2 to 3 minutes until saucy, a little messy and luscious.

6. Sprinkle goat cheese crumbles evenly over the mixture, and fold into the polenta once or twice. Remove from heat when the cheese starts to melt, usually within 1 minute. Serve garnished with chopped herb(s) and bits of chopped olives.

Three-Cheese Polenta

SERVES 4 TO 6

*Here's another recipe for
polenta, this time marrying
the wholesome cornmeal
pudding with three cheeses,
tomato, garlic and olives for
a high-voltage combination
that will warm a winter-weary
heart and — a warning
here — puts pounds where
one might not want them.
Calories notwithstanding, I
recommend this dish highly
for its taste, especially when
accompanied by some red
wine and followed by a green
salad. Ease of preparation
also recommends it — the
dish can be prepared in
advance and baked later. It
can also be baked through
and reheated (even the next
day) without much loss of
moisture or flavor.*

✳ ✳ ✳

PREHEAT OVEN TO 375°F (190°C)
DEEP 6- TO 8-CUP (1.5 TO 2 L) CASSEROLE DISH

2½ cups	water	625 mL
½ tsp	salt	2 mL
1 cup	yellow cornmeal	250 mL
2 tbsp	olive oil	25 mL
1 tbsp	finely chopped garlic	15 mL
½ tsp	hot pepper flakes	2 mL
¼ tsp	salt	1 mL
¼ tsp	freshly ground black pepper	1 mL
12 oz	plum tomatoes, peeled and roughly chopped or 2 cups (500 mL) canned	375 g
½ tsp	dried basil leaves	2 mL
½ tsp	dried oregano leaves	2 mL
1 tsp	balsamic vinegar	5 mL
4	sun-dried tomatoes, finely sliced	4
4	black olives, pitted and chopped	4
6 oz	low-fat ricotta cheese	175 g
4 oz	Gorgonzola cheese	125 g
3 oz	full-bodied Italian cheese such as Crotonese, Provolone, Parmesan, shredded	90 g
	Few sprigs fresh basil, chopped	

1. In a large deep saucepan, bring water to a rolling boil. Add salt. Reduce heat to low. Add cornmeal in a thin but steady stream, stirring constantly (preferably with a wooden spoon). Cook, stirring, for 2 to 3 minutes or until the mixture is smooth and has thickened to the consistency of mashed potatoes. Transfer polenta to a medium bowl and cover with an inverted plate. Let rest at least 10 minutes.

2. Meanwhile, in a frying pan, heat olive oil over high heat for 1 minute. Add garlic, hot pepper flakes, salt and pepper; stir-fry for 1 minute or until garlic starts to brown. Immediately add tomatoes, basil, oregano and vinegar; stir-fry for 2 minutes or until tomatoes break down and a sauce forms. Remove from heat.

3. Turn the cooled polenta onto plate by inverting the bowl and giving it a small tap. Spread a small quantity of tomato sauce on the bottom of casserole. Cut polenta in half; cut each half into slices $\frac{1}{4}$ to $\frac{1}{2}$ inch (0.5 cm to 1 cm) thick. Place half of polenta slices on top of the smear of sauce to make a layer. Scatter sun-dried tomato and olive bits on this layer of polenta. Spread all the sauce evenly. Dot dollops of ricotta and Gorgonzola evenly over the sauce. Place remaining polenta slices on top of cheeses. Scatter the shredded Italian cheese on top of polenta. (The recipe can be prepared in advance to this point and wait up to 2 hours, covered and unrefrigerated.)

4. Bake in preheated oven, uncovered, for 30 minutes or until lightly browned and piping hot right through. Remove from oven and let rest for 5 minutes. Scoop out portions onto plates, getting some of the shredded cheese layer up top. Garnish with chopped fresh basil and serve immediately.

Eggplant Pilaf

SERVES 8

Another of my family's heirloom recipes, this enhanced rice dish will complement any number of vegetable side dishes. If you're not vegan, it can even make a nice lunch on its own, if you don't stint on the Cucumber Raita accompaniment. This recipe is based on using an entire, regular-size eggplant. The recipe can be easily halved if you don't mind using only half an eggplant.

❊ ❊ ❊

Tip

Be sure to wash leek thoroughly, splitting down the middle and paying special care to the grit that hides where the green and white parts meet.

4 cups	unpeeled, diced eggplant (about 1 medium)	1 L
1 tbsp	salt	15 mL
2 tbsp	olive oil	25 mL
1 tsp	salt	5 mL
½ tsp	freshly ground black pepper	2 mL
½ tsp	turmeric	2 mL
2	cloves	2
Pinch	ground cumin	Pinch
1	onion, finely diced	1
1 cup	finely chopped leek (1 medium)	250 mL
4	cloves garlic, minced	4
2 cups	rice (preferably basmati)	500 mL
3 cups	boiling water	750 mL
¼ cup	olive oil	50 mL
	Cucumber Raita (see recipe, page 167) (optional)	

1. Place the cubed eggplant and salt in bowl; add cold water to cover. Mix well and set aside.

2. In a heavy-bottomed pot with a tight-fitting lid, heat 2 tbsp (25 mL) oil over high heat for 30 seconds. Add salt, black pepper, turmeric, cloves and cumin; stir for 30 seconds. Add onions and stir-fry for 1 minute. Add chopped leek and continue stir-frying for 1 minute. Add garlic and stir-fry for 30 seconds.

3. Add rice and stir-fry until grains are shiny, about 1 to 2 minutes. (Don't worry if the spices start to scorch on the bottom of the pan; the next addition will cure that.)

4. Add boiling water, and pull pot off heat as it sizzles and splutters for 30 seconds. Reduce heat to low; return pot to heat, cover tightly and let it simmer for 20 minutes. Then remove from heat but do not uncover. Let rice mixture rest for 10 minutes to temper.

5. Meanwhile, in a large frying pan, heat ¼ cup (50 mL) oil over high heat for 1 minute. Drain eggplant cubes and add to oil (carefully: there will be spluttering). Fry for 6 to 7 minutes, stirring and tossing actively, until all the cubes have softened and have started to brown. Remove from heat and set aside.

6. Fluff rice and add fried eggplant, folding from the bottom up to distribute the eggplant, as well as the onions and leeks that will have risen to the top of the rice. Transfer to a presentation dish and serve immediately with a side bowl of Cucumber Raita as an accompaniment, if desired.

Mushroom Risotto

SERVES 4

Despite the widely perceived difficulty of creating a successful risotto, there really is no rice dish that can touch it for sheer taste and comfort. Let's remove the anxiety: risottos are failproof as long as the minimum of care is afforded them (and your heat is not too high).

As for all the stirring required — well, think of it as an excellent opportunity for reflection or inspiration. (Rossini is said to have composed his best arias while stirring his risotti.) This recipe is from fellow foodie and excellent friend, Amnon Medad. It uses no cream, but manages to turn out creamy and very smooth.

✻ ✻ ✻

3 tbsp	butter	45 mL
¼ tsp	salt	1 mL
¼ tsp	freshly ground black pepper	1 mL
3 cups	sliced mushrooms (wild or regular)	750 mL
1 tbsp	freshly squeezed lemon juice	15 mL
4 cups	Mushroom Stock (see recipe, page 53)	1 L
¼ cup	butter	50 mL
½ cup	finely diced onion	125 mL
¼ cup	finely diced celery leaves and/or stalks	50 mL
3	cloves garlic, finely chopped	3
2 tbsp	finely chopped fresh parsley	25 mL
1 tsp	dried tarragon	5 mL
1 cup	short-grain rice (Arborio or Vialone Nano)	250 mL
½ tsp	salt	2 mL
1 cup	dry white wine	250 mL
	Few sprigs fresh parsley, chopped	
	Freshly ground black pepper to taste	
	Grated Pecorino or Parmesan cheese (optional)	

1. In a large frying pan, melt 3 tbsp (45 mL) butter over high heat for 1 minute until sizzling. Add salt and pepper and stir. Add sliced mushrooms and stir-fry for 5 to 6 minutes until browned. Remove from heat, stir in lemon juice and set aside.

2. In a saucepan, gradually warm mushroom stock over low heat until very hot. Do not boil.

3. Meanwhile, in a heavy-bottomed pot, melt ¼ cup (50 mL) butter over medium heat for 1 to 2 minutes until it starts to sizzle. Add onions and celery; stir-fry for 4 to 5 minutes until softened. Add garlic, parsley and tarragon and stir-fry for 1 minute. Add rice and salt and increase heat to high. Vigorously stir-fry the rice for 3 to 4 minutes until it is coated with butter and thoroughly hot.

4. Add wine and stir-cook for about 3 minutes until all the liquid has been absorbed/evaporated and the rice starts to look dry. Reduce heat to medium and add about ¹⁄₂ cup (125 mL) of the hot mushroom stock. Stir, then wait until the liquid starts to bubble and rise above the rice. Let it cook for another minute and stir. Wait for liquid to rise again, let cook another minute and stir. Repeat wait-cook-stir cycle until the liquid has been mostly absorbed and the rice begins to appear dry.

5. Add another ¹⁄₂ cup (125 mL) of the mushroom stock and repeat the wait-cook-stir cycle until the rice is beautifully cooked (still al dente, but with a very tender interior). You may not need to use all of the stock. The entire process should take about 25 to 35 minutes.

6. Add reserved mushrooms and any pan juices to the rice; stir and cook for 1 minute. Remove from heat, cover and let it rest for 5 minutes to absorb excess moisture. Serve garnished with some chopped parsley and freshly cracked pepper. The cheese is truly optional. It tends to mask several of the risotto's lovely flavors, but some people simply can't enjoy it without its cheese.

Levantine Rice

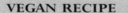

SERVES 4 TO 6

A perfect rice for entertaining, this slightly sweet yet savory pilaf can be enjoyed warm or at room temperature, and robustly accompanies just about anything you wish to serve with it (especially if from the eastern half of the Mediterranean basin). The recipe can be multiplied at will to accommodate large party buffets.

❋ ❋ ❋

¼ cup	olive oil	50 mL
¼ tsp	salt	1 mL
¼ tsp	freshly ground black pepper	1 mL
½ tsp	ground cinnamon	2 mL
2	onions, finely diced	2
1 cup	short-grain rice (preferably Arborio or Vialone Nano)	250 mL
½ tsp	granulated sugar	2 mL
2 tbsp	raisins	25 mL
1¾ cups	boiling water	425 mL
⅓ cup	toasted pine nuts	75 mL
	Few sprigs fresh parsley, chopped	

1. In a heavy-bottomed pot with a tight-fitting lid, heat oil over high heat for 30 seconds. Add salt, pepper and cinnamon and stir-fry for just under 1 minute, until cinnamon darkens. Add onions and stir-fry for 2 minutes until softened.

2. Add rice and stir-fry actively for 3 minutes, until all of it has been exposed to the oil and is heated through. Add sugar and raisins and stir to mix.

3. Immediately add boiling water (use ¼ cup/50 mL less water if you like rice al dente), and pull pot off heat as it sizzles and splutters for 30 seconds. Mix well and reduce heat to low. Cover pot tightly. Let simmer undisturbed for 20 minutes, then remove from heat; do not uncover, but let it rest for 10 minutes to temper. (For up to 30 or 40 minutes, it will stay warm and improve.)

4. When ready to serve, fluff the rice, folding from the bottom up to redistribute the onions that have risen to the top, and transfer to a serving dish. Garnish liberally with pine nuts and parsley.

Sauces & Condiments

❁

Hot Oil

**MAKES ABOUT
⅓ CUP (75 ML)**

*Greeks, like me, are well
known for loving oil so much
that they garnish their oil
with more oil — hot, flavored
oil, that is. Here are two
recipes for hot oil, one Asian
for spicing up savories like
the Asian Spring Rolls (see
recipe, page 42) and Don
Don Noodles (see recipe,
page 84), and one based
on olive oil for just about
everything else (especially
pastas and pizzas).*

**MAKES ABOUT
⅓ CUP (75 ML)**

Tip
Both types of oil can be
made ahead and kept,
covered and refrigerated,
for up to several days.

Le-chou-yao (Asian Hot Oil)

¼ cup	vegetable oil	50 mL
1 tsp	hot pepper flakes	5 mL
1 tbsp	soy sauce	15 mL

1. In a small saucepan, heat vegetable oil over high heat until it's just about to smoke, about 1 to 2 minutes. Remove from heat and add hot pepper flakes; they will sizzle and darken. (If they turn black, then your oil is too hot: start again.) Add soy sauce and take cover: it'll splatter for 5 to 10 seconds. When it subsides, stir once and transfer to a serving bowl.

Hot Olive Oil

¼ cup	olive oil	50 mL
2	cloves garlic, lightly crushed, but not pressed	2
1 tsp	hot pepper flakes	5 mL
1 tsp	balsamic vinegar	5 mL

1. In a small saucepan, heat olive oil over high heat for 30 seconds. Add garlic; cook for 1 to 2 minutes or until garlic has started to brown. Remove from heat; remove and discard garlic.

2. Immediately add hot pepper flakes; they will sizzle and darken. Add vinegar and take cover: it'll splatter for 5 to 10 seconds. When it subsides, stir once and transfer to a serving bowl.

Linguine Barolo (page 140)

Vinaigrette

**MAKES ABOUT
½ CUP (125 ML)**

*The premier salad dressing
in the world, this is oil and
vinegar at its best. Ideal
for all types of salads and
greens, it is also a light
and easy dip for things
like asparagus.*

✹ ✹ ✹

Tip
This dressing can be
made in advance and
refrigerated or left out
covered. It must be
whisked to re-emulsify
before serving.

2 tbsp	minced shallots or red onion	25 mL
1 tbsp	French mustard, whole-grain or smooth	15 mL
1 tbsp	white wine vinegar	15 mL
1 tbsp	pressed garlic	15 mL
¼ cup	extra virgin olive oil	50 mL
	Few sprigs fresh tarragon and/or parsley, chopped	
	Salt and freshly ground black pepper to taste	

1. In a bowl, whisk together shallots, mustard, vinegar
and garlic. Add olive oil in a thin stream, whisking
all the while, until it is emulsified. Add chopped
herbs and whisk until blended. Season to taste with
salt and pepper.

Baked Peaches
with Almond Crust (page 182)

Aïoli (Garlic Mayonnaise)

MAKES ABOUT 1¼ CUPS (300 ML)

The advent of food processors has obviated the need for store-bought mayonnaise. What used to take an eternity of elbow grease in the days of whisks can now be achieved in almost no time (if we don't count washing up). This dressing is particularly wonderful on salads of slightly bitter greens like watercress, endive and escarole. On the other hand, it works very well on soft greens like Boston and butter lettuce.

※ ※ ※

Tip

As an accompaniment to dishes like soups, use the aïoli as is. For salad dressings, whisk in 3 to 4 tbsp (45 to 60 mL) cold water, 1 tbsp (15 mL) at a time, until desired consistency is achieved.

2	egg yolks	2
2 tbsp	freshly squeezed lemon juice	25 mL
1 tbsp	pressed garlic	15 mL
1 tbsp	red wine vinegar	15 mL
1 tsp	Dijon mustard	5 mL
1 cup	extra virgin olive oil	250 mL
	Salt and freshly ground black pepper to taste	

1. In a food processor, blend egg yolks at high speed for 30 seconds until color lightens. Add lemon juice, garlic, vinegar and mustard. Process at high until mixture is frothy.

2. While food processor continues to run at high speed, add olive oil through the feed tube in droplets at first, then in a thin stream. The sauce will turn quite thick after 1 cup (250 mL) of oil has been added.

3. Transfer mayonnaise to a bowl. Season to taste with salt and pepper. The aïoli will keep for 2 to 3 days, covered and refrigerated.

Sesame Dressing

MAKES ABOUT
1 CUP (250 ML)

A light and aromatic salad dressing, it's made with Chinese sesame sauce, the brown sesame-seed paste that is available in all Asian markets. This tahini-like bottled substance is usually quite dense, with an inch or so of oil separated and risen to the top. In this recipe it is crucial to use some of the oil along with the solids (a ratio of 1 part oil to 4 parts solids is about right). This dressing can be used on a green salad, but is most effective with blanched and/or raw vegetables like broccoli, carrot, snow peas and bean sprouts.

※ ※ ※

Tip

This dressing can be made in advance and kept covered. It'll solidify in the fridge, but will soften when it reaches room temperature and is re-whisked. Serve alongside salad to be added at table; it tends to dry on the surface if vegetables are pre-tossed.

3 tbsp	Chinese sesame sauce	45 mL
½ cup	warm water	125 mL
1 tbsp	minced gingerroot	15 mL
2	green onions, finely chopped	2
2 tbsp	rice vinegar or lime juice	25 mL
1 to 3 tsp	soy sauce	5 to 15 mL

1. Spoon out sesame sauce from its jar, including a bit of the oil, and transfer to a small bowl. Prod the solids with a fork until slightly loosened, then whisk in warm water, a little at a time. (The mixture will appear hopelessly lumpy at first, but gives up resistance after 2 to 3 minutes of whisking and becomes very smooth.) Add ginger, green onions, rice vinegar and soy sauce to taste. Whisk into the sesame sauce for 1 minute to blend well.

Pico De Gallo
(Mexican Hot Sauce)

MAKES ABOUT
1 CUP (250 ML)

This delicious, versatile and explosive sauce requires no cooking, and can live in the fridge nicely for two to three days, though it is best about an hour after it's freshly made. The hotness of the sauce can be regulated by modifying the amount of jalapeño pepper seeds used.

Tip

When working with hot peppers, be sure to wear gloves; otherwise, wash hands thoroughly.

1	medium tomato, cut into 1/4-inch (0.5 cm) cubes	1
1/4 cup	finely diced red onion	50 mL
2	jalapeño peppers, finely diced (with or without seeds, depending on desired hotness)	2
1/2 tsp	salt	2 mL
1 tbsp	lime juice	15 mL
1 tbsp	vegetable oil	15 mL
	Few sprigs fresh coriander, chopped	

1. In a bowl, combine tomato, onions, jalapeño, salt and lime juice. Stir to mix well. Add oil and stir again.

2. Transfer to a serving bowl and scatter chopped coriander on top. Let rest for about 1 hour, covered and unrefrigerated, for best flavor. Serve alongside main courses and appetizers.

Salsa Cynthia

**MAKES ABOUT
2 CUPS (500 ML)**

*This salsa is perfect as a
dip for nachos, and as
an accompaniment to
Mexican-style dishes like
enchiladas, as well as
avocado-based salsas and
soups. I dedicate this recipe
to my friend, Cynthia Good,
who likes things hot.*

※ ※ ※

Tips

The flavor of this sauce
improves if kept in the
fridge for up to 3 or
4 days. Stir thoroughly
before each use.

When working with hot
peppers, be sure to wear
gloves; otherwise, wash
hands thoroughly.

4	ripe tomatoes	4
1	red or white onion, cut into eighths	1
2	cloves garlic, crushed	2
Pinch	salt	Pinch
5	jalapeño peppers	5
2 tbsp	vegetable oil	25 mL
1 tbsp	lime juice	15 mL
	Few sprigs fresh coriander, chopped	

1. Blanch tomatoes in boiling water for 30 seconds.
   Over a bowl, peel, core and deseed them. Chop
   tomatoes roughly and put in a food processor. Strain
   any accumulated tomato juices from bowl; add to
   food processor. Add onion pieces, garlic and salt.

2. Remove the stems of the jalapeños, and cut them
   into halves. Scoop out and discard the core and most
   of the seeds (the more seeds, the hotter your sauce;
   without any seeds, you'll have a mildly hot sauce).
   Chop the peppers roughly and add to the food
   processor, along with retained seeds. Pulse on and
   off until mixed and slightly chunky, but not puréed.

3. Transfer mixture to a saucepan, add vegetable oil,
   and cook over medium heat for 6 to 8 minutes, until
   mildly bubbling and foaming pinkly. Remove from
   heat and let salsa cool for at least 10 minutes.

4. Add lime juice and chopped coriander; stir well and
   serve.

Tzatziki Sauce

MAKES 1 1/3 CUPS (325 ML)

A relative (and a descendant) of Afghani/Indian raitas, this soothing-yet-exciting yogurt-based sauce is a lovely complement to Greek-style fried zucchini and a wonderful dip for raw vegetables. In fact, you can use it to provide an additional taste sensation to any Mediterranean recipe. It's best when made ahead, and keeps nicely in the refrigerator for up to three days (after that it gets too garlicky). If refrigerated, it must be brought back up to room temperature.

1/2 cup	peeled, coarsely shredded English cucumber	125 mL
1 cup	yogurt	250 mL
2	cloves garlic	2
	Salt to taste	
1 tsp	extra virgin olive oil	5 mL
Pinch	cayenne pepper or paprika	Pinch

1. Drain cucumber through a strainer, pressing by hand to extract as much juice as possible (you can save this juice and use it as an astringent for the face).

2. In a bowl, stir together cucumber shreds and yogurt. Press garlic through a garlic press directly into bowl; mix in. Season to taste with salt.

3. Transfer sauce to a serving bowl and let rest for 30 minutes. Drizzle olive oil on it and sprinkle cayenne (for spicy) or paprika (for mild) just before serving.

Cucumber Raita

**MAKES 2 CUPS
(500 ML)**

*A multi-use, India-inspired
sauce, this is a must with
highly spiced dishes (as
a cooler), as it is with
weightier items like pies
(as a picker-upper). It even
works as a chunky dip for
raw veggies or corn chips.*

1 cup	yogurt	250 mL
1 ⅓ cups	unpeeled, finely diced English cucumber	325 mL
2 tbsp	finely chopped fresh mint or 1 tbsp (15 mL) dried	25 mL
1 tbsp	freshly squeezed lemon juice	15 mL
1 tsp	vegetable oil	5 mL
	Salt to taste	
½ tsp	garam masala	2 mL

1. In a bowl, combine yogurt and cucumber. Stir in mint, lemon juice and oil. Season to taste with salt; mix thoroughly.

2. Transfer to a serving bowl and sprinkle garam masala on the surface (do not mix in). Let rest unrefrigerated for 30 minutes and serve.

Mango Raita

MAKES 1²⁄₃ CUPS (400 ML)

This refreshing, fruity yogurt sauce is a must-serve with all East Indian meals. It puts out the chili-fires and painlessly enriches the main dishes.

Variation

A green apple or peach can replace the mango.

1	ripe mango	1
1 cup	yogurt	250 mL
1 tsp	garam masala	5 mL
	Vegetable oil	

1. Working over a bowl to catch any juices, peel the mango and dice flesh into ¹⁄₂-inch (1 cm) cubes. Stir in yogurt.

2. Transfer to a serving bowl; sprinkle with garam masala and a few drops of oil. Let rest unrefrigerated for 30 minutes, and serve.

Desserts

Baked Ricotta Meenakshi

MAKES 16 SQUARES

Meenakshi, chef and all-around-famous inhabitant of Taos, New Mexico, invented this charmingly simple dessert as a finale to her popular Indian meals. It approximates the taste and texture of authentic Indian sweets such as rasmalai, *but with half the sugar and much less fat.*

❈ ❈ ❈

PREHEAT OVEN TO 325°F (160°C)
8-INCH (20 CM) SQUARE BAKING PAN,
GENEROUSLY GREASED WITH VEGETABLE SHORTENING

2 cups	ricotta cheese	500 mL
¾ cup	icing sugar	175 mL
1 tbsp	ground cardamom	15 mL
¼ cup	whipping (35%) cream	50 mL
¼ cup	shelled, skinned pistachios, divided	50 mL

1. Put ricotta in a bowl, and sift icing sugar over it. Sprinkle evenly with cardamom. Using a wooden spoon, beat mixture until well integrated. Transfer to baking pan and smooth the surface.

2. Bake ricotta mixture for 1 hour until it is lightly browned, about half its original height, and feels firm to the touch. Remove from oven and let cool for 30 to 60 minutes.

3. Cut into 2-inch (5 cm) squares. Lift pieces carefully and arrange on a dessert platter. Top each square with a little of the heavy cream. Crush half the pistachios and sprinkle on top. Use the rest of the pistachios whole to garnish (or decorate) the squares. Serve immediately.

Wrenn's Ricotta Pie

SERVES 8 TO 12

Cooking for a film crew over a number of weeks while stuck in an exotic location (like the wilds of Newfoundland) means having to come up with new desserts every day. And when you run out of ideas — as I did — it's no laughing matter. An emergency phone call to Wrenn Goodrum in New York produced this lovely, no-bake cheesecake, reminiscent of Italian cannoli, without the fuss. It's not exactly diet material, but then again what proper dessert is?

❋ ❋ ❋

Tip

For a creamier texture, use the smooth variety of ricotta.

PREHEAT OVEN TO 350°F (180°C)
12-INCH (30 CM) ROUND BAKING DISH, GREASED WITH BUTTER

1 cup	graham cracker crumbs	250 mL
¼ cup	unsalted butter, melted	50 mL
1 tbsp	granulated sugar	15 mL
2 cups	ricotta cheese (see Tip, left)	500 mL
¼ cup	granulated sugar	50 mL
¾ cup	toasted slivered almonds, divided	175 mL
½ cup	bittersweet chocolate chips	125 mL
1 tbsp	amaretto liqueur	15 mL
½ cup	whipping (35%) cream	125 mL

1. In a bowl, combine graham cracker crumbs, butter and sugar; mix to a mealy, paste-like texture. Transfer the crumb mixture into the baking dish and press it down to cover the entire bottom (no need to do the sides). Bake for 10 to 12 minutes until slightly browned. Remove from oven and let cool down completely, about 45 minutes.

2. Meanwhile, in another bowl, combine ricotta and sugar; mix with a spoon to blend thoroughly.

3. In a food processor, grind half the toasted almonds, until coarse meal. Add ground almonds to the ricotta mixture, and beat with a spoon to distribute. Add chocolate chips and amaretto. Beat well, until the mixture has become smooth, soft and thoroughly blended.

4. Add whipping cream to a chilled bowl and beat until stiff; add cream to the ricotta mixture, folding it in gently but thoroughly.

5. Transfer mixture to the graham crust, smoothing it to fill the pan evenly. Garnish with remaining almond slivers, cover with plastic wrap and refrigerate for at least 2 hours until the cheese has stiffened. Serve cold.

Individual Apple Strudel

SERVES 6

Phyllo dough works so well for strudel, you'd swear the stuff was invented for it. I've enriched this basic recipe with pecans, which lend a sun-belt warmth that is particularly welcome when this dessert is served in winter.

❋ ❋ ❋

Tips

Use any variety of apples. To avoid browning, add the apple slices to the orange-lemon juice immediately after peeling and slicing them.

Leftovers can be kept covered and unrefrigerated. Warm them slightly before serving.

PREHEAT OVEN TO 350°F (180°C)
BAKING SHEET, LIGHTLY GREASED WITH BUTTER

¼ cup	orange juice	50 mL
1 tbsp	freshly squeezed lemon juice	15 mL
1 lb	apples, peeled, cored and cut into thin slices (about 4 apples) (see Tips, left)	500 g
2 tbsp	cornstarch	25 mL
1 cup	toasted pecans	250 mL
⅓ cup	raisins	75 mL
3 tbsp	packed brown sugar	45 mL
1 tsp	ground cinnamon	5 mL
½ tsp	ground nutmeg	2 mL
½ tsp	ground clove	2 mL
12	sheets phyllo dough	12
½ cup	unsalted butter, melted	125 mL

1. In a bowl, mix together orange and lemon juices. Add apple slices and fold to cover with juice. Sprinkle apples with cornstarch and mix well. Add pecans, raisins, sugar, cinnamon, nutmeg and clove; mix gently but thoroughly.

2. On a dry surface lay out a sheet of phyllo and brush with melted butter. Cover with a second sheet of phyllo and brush with butter. Transfer one-sixth of the apple mixture (about ¾ cup/175 mL) to the upper center of the buttered phyllo sheet. Fold the top flap over the filling and fold both vertical sides to the inside, as if shaping an envelope. Roll the stuffed end down, to create a plump rectangular pie, measuring about 4 by 2 inches (10 by 5 cm). Transfer pie to prepared baking sheet and repeat filling procedure for 5 remaining pies. Brush remaining melted butter on the tops and sides of pies.

3. Bake in preheated oven for 15 to 20 minutes until the phyllo has turned golden brown and crisp. Remove from oven and let cool at least 10 minutes before serving with vanilla ice cream on the side (if calories permit).

Marion's Almond-Chocolate Torte

SERVES 8

This deeply almondy cake is the brainchild of my good friend Marion Medad, who hails from one of the world's most gourmet families. She substitutes 8 oz (250 g) of marzipan for my ground almonds, which makes the torte fudgier, but more difficult to serve. Either way, get ready for the compliments.

Tip

This torte will live nicely, unrefrigerated and lightly covered, for up to 2 days. The raspberry coulis can be made ahead and kept, covered and refrigerated, for up to 5 days.

PREHEAT OVEN TO 350°F (180°C)
10-INCH (25 CM) PIE PLATE, LIGHTLY OILED AND DUSTED WITH FLOUR

Torte

1 1/2 cups	ground almonds (about 6 oz/175 g)	375 mL
3/4 cup	granulated sugar	175 mL
1/2 cup	unsalted butter, melted	125 mL
3	eggs, beaten	3
2 tbsp	amaretto	25 mL
1/4 tsp	almond extract	1 mL
1/3 cup	cocoa powder	75 mL
1/2 tsp	baking powder	2 mL
	Icing sugar	

Raspberry Coulis

10 oz	frozen raspberries, thawed	300 g
1/2 cup	granulated sugar	125 mL

1. Put ground almonds into a food processor. Add sugar and melted butter; process until blended and forming into a ball. Add beaten eggs, amaretto and almond extract; process until like very thick cream. Sift cocoa powder and baking powder into food processor. Process with several pulses until just blended.
2. Transfer mixture to pie plate, tapping plate a couple of times to settle its contents. Bake in preheated oven for 30 to 35 minutes until top has crusted, the sides have pulled in a little and cake tester comes out dry. Remove from oven and let cool down completely in the pie plate (the center will cave in very slightly). Dust top with icing sugar.
3. Make the coulis: In a saucepan, heat raspberries over medium heat until they start to foam, about 5 to 7 minutes. Add sugar and stir until dissolved. Reduce heat and simmer for 15 minutes, stirring occasionally. Strain coulis into a bowl, discarding the seeds. Let cool.
4. Serve wedges of torte directly from pie plate onto a pool of coulis.

Aristedes' Bougatsa

SERVES 4

The Canadian-Greek superchef Aristedes has invented close to 800 dishes for the menus of his 40 restaurants in Canada and the U.S. Though I've loved a great number of them, the one I always crave is this simple custard pie, a contemporary embellishment of a traditional Greek dessert. Here it is as related to me by Aristedes' long-time lieutenant and sous-chef, Kenny Brudner.

Tip

Leftovers can be kept covered and refrigerated. Heat them to lukewarm before serving.

PREHEAT OVEN TO 350°F (180°C)
BAKING SHEET, LIGHTLY GREASED WITH BUTTER

2 cups	homogenized milk	500 mL
1/2 cup	granulated sugar	125 mL
1 tbsp	orange zest	15 mL
1 tbsp	lemon zest	15 mL
1/2 tsp	vanilla extract	2 mL
3 tbsp	unsalted butter	45 mL
1/2 cup	semolina	125 mL
8	sheets phyllo dough	8
3 tbsp	melted unsalted butter	45 mL
	Pieces of fruit such as sliced mango or pear, berries, etc.	
	Ground cinnamon	

1. In a saucepan over low heat, combine milk, sugar, orange and lemon zest and vanilla. Heat slowly for about 10 minutes, until hot but not boiling.
2. Meanwhile, in a small frying pan, melt butter over medium heat. Add semolina and stir into a paste. Cook for 2 minutes, stirring continuously. Remove from heat.
3. Add about one-quarter of the semolina mixture to the hot milk and whisk to incorporate. Proceed with the rest of the semolina, one-quarter at a time, until it is all in and whisked into a thick custard. Continue simmering for 3 to 4 minutes, whisking vigorously until quite stiff. Remove from heat, and let cool down completely, about 30 minutes.

4. On a dry surface lay out a sheet of phyllo and brush with melted butter. Cover with a second sheet of phyllo and brush with butter. Transfer ¼ of the custard (about ½ cup/125 mL) to the upper center of the buttered phyllo sheet and stud the custard with a few pieces of fruit. Fold the top flap over the filling and fold both vertical sides to the inside, as if shaping an envelope. Roll the stuffed end down to create a plump rectangular pie, measuring about 4 by 2 inches (10 by 5 cm). Transfer pie to baking sheet and repeat filling procedure for 3 remaining pies. Brush remaining melted butter on the tops and sides of pies.

5. Bake in preheated oven for 15 to 20 minutes until the phyllo has turned golden brown and crisp. Remove from oven and let cool about 10 minutes. Serve lukewarm sprinkled with cinnamon.

Hazelnut Baklava

SERVES 16

Baklava need not be the
dense, ludicrously syruped
layers of endless phyllo
dough with a thin layer
of nuts somewhere in the
middle. It can also be
airy, intensely nutty and
minimally moistened with
honey, as is the case with
the varied shapes of Middle
Eastern baklavas. I've
simplified the shape but
retained the crunch of the
latter, a result of slow baking,
and bold use of various
nuts. The combination of
hazelnuts (filberts) and
pistachios (my preference)
can be substituted with
other nuts such as almonds,
walnuts — even peanuts.

✳ ✳ ✳

PREHEAT OVEN TO 275°F (140°C)
16-BY 10-INCH (45 BY 25 CM) RECTANGULAR BAKING DISH,
LIGHTLY BUTTERED

½ cup	roasted hazelnuts (filberts), skinned (about 7 oz/190 g) (see Tip, right)	125 mL
½ cup	shelled, skinned pistachios (about 3 oz/90 g)	125 mL
⅔ cup	granulated sugar	150 mL
1 tbsp	ground cinnamon	15 mL
8	sheets phyllo dough	8
½ cup	unsalted butter, melted	125 mL
½ cup	liquid honey	125 mL
½ cup	hot water	125 mL

1. In a food processor, combine hazelnuts, pistachios, sugar and cinnamon. Process at high speed for less than 1 minute, until nuts are ground to the consistency of coarse meal, with a few chunks remaining intact.

2. On a dry working surface, lay out a sheet of phyllo, short side towards you. Using a pastry brush lightly butter the half nearest you. Fold the unbuttered half over and lightly butter the fresh surface. (You'll now have a double layer of phyllo, buttered in-between and above.) Sprinkle 3 tbsp (45 mL) of the nut mixture evenly over the entire phyllo surface. Roll the stuffed phyllo away from you, forming a long tubular shape, a bit more than 1 inch (2.5 cm) wide. This rolling should be as tight as possible, but loose enough not to tear the phyllo. Place this tube against one of the walls of the baking dish.

3. Repeat procedure with remaining 7 sheets of phyllo, fitting the new tubes snugly against each other, but without squeezing. When all 8 baklavas have been rolled, they'll fill out the entire pan. There should be just enough butter left over to brush the entire top surface of all the baklavas. This final buttering is very important: if you've run out of butter, then melt some more.

4. Bake in preheated oven for about 1 hour until browned and their surfaces are very crisp. Remove from oven. Immediately heat honey and water together, stirring until almost bubbling. Spoon the hot honey-water mixture evenly over the warm baklavas and leave alone for about 1 hour.

5. The baklavas can be served at this point or they can sit for up to 2 days, unrefrigerated and lightly covered. Serve half a tube per person, either as is, or cut on the bias into 2 or 3 pieces.

Walnut-Chocolate Baklava

SERVES 16

The addition of chocolate gives a new taste to baklava and I thought we should offer a recipe before everyone else does it. Here I use the same slow-cooked, sparely used phyllo way that I make all my baklavas. It is just more airy and crunchy than with the more traditional layered-pie method — closer to the feeling of a Middle Eastern baklava than a Greek one. The better the quality of chocolate you use, the more delicious it'll end up (obviously), but commercial chocolate chips will work, as long as they are semisweet.

✳ ✳ ✳

PREHEAT OVEN TO 275°F (140°C)
16-BY 10-INCH (45 BY 25 CM) RECTANGULAR BAKING DISH, LIGHTLY BUTTERED

1 1/4 cups	walnut pieces	300 mL
7 oz	bittersweet chocolate, chopped	200 g
8	sheets phyllo dough	8
1/2 cup	unsalted butter, melted	125 mL
1/2 cup	granulated sugar	125 mL
1/2 cup	water	125 mL

1. In a food processor, combine walnuts and chocolate pieces at high speed for about 1 minute or until nuts and chocolate are ground to the consistency of coarse meal, with some little chunks left.

2. On a dry working surface, lay out a sheet of phyllo, short side towards you. Using a pastry brush lightly butter the half nearest you. Fold the unbuttered half over and lightly butter the fresh surface. (You'll now have a double layer of phyllo, buttered in-between and above.) Sprinkle 1/4 cup (50 mL) of the walnut-chocolate mixture evenly over the entire phyllo surface. Roll the stuffed phyllo away from you, forming a long tubular shape, a bit more than 1 inch (2.5 cm) wide. This rolling should be as tight as possible, but loose enough so as not to tear the phyllo. Place this tube against one of the walls of the baking dish.

3. Repeat procedure with remaining 7 sheets of phyllo, fitting the new tubes snugly against each other, but without squeezing. When all 8 baklavas have been rolled, they'll fill out the entire pan. There should be just enough butter left over to brush the entire top surface of all the baklavas. This final buttering is very important; if you've run out of butter, then melt some more.

4. Bake in preheated oven for about 1 hour or until browned and surfaces are very crisp. Remove from oven. In a small pan, combine sugar and water; bring to a boil (no need to stir, the sugar melts itself). Reduce heat to medium; cook for 3 minutes or until slightly thickened. Pour hot syrup evenly over the warm baklavas. Let rest for 1 hour.

5. The baklavas can be served at this point or they can sit for up to 2 days, unrefrigerated and lightly covered. Serve half a tube per person, either as is, or cut on the bias into 2 or 3 pieces.

Fried Pineapple

SERVES 4

Here's one for those occasions when you're short of time but still feel like a good dessert. With staples such as sugar, unsalted butter, good raisins and bittersweet chocolate in your larder, all you need from the store is a ripe pineapple, and then 10 minutes of quick and easy work.

❋ ❋ ❋

1	ripe pineapple	1
2 tbsp	granulated sugar	25 mL
2 tbsp	unsalted butter	25 mL
2 tbsp	sultana raisins	25 mL
1 oz	bittersweet chocolate, shaved	30 g
4	sprigs fresh mint	4

1. With a sharp knife cut off top half of pineapple, reserving it for another use. Remove rind from the bottom (sweeter) half and slice pineapple into 4 rounds, each ½ inch (1 cm) thick. Spread sugar on a plate and dredge the pineapple slices in the sugar.

2. In a large frying pan, melt butter over high heat until foaming. Add the dredged pineapple slices and fry for 2 minutes. Flip the slices and spread raisins around them; fry for another 2 to 3 minutes until pineapple has browned and raisins are swollen. Remove from heat and transfer one pineapple slice to each of 4 dessert plates, flipping them so the more attractively browned side faces upward. Spoon some raisins onto each plate and top with a bit of the sauce from the pan. Garnish with chocolate shavings and mint. Serve immediately.

Chocolate Fondue

SERVES 2

*This one is for lovers.
The two of you can invoke
St. Valentine any day of
the year with a pot of
melted chocolate, some
fruit, biscuits and
a lot of affection.*

※ ※ ※

4 oz	fine chocolate, preferably bittersweet, broken into pieces	125 g
2 tbsp	Frangelico liqueur	25 mL
1 tbsp	water	15 mL
	Assorted imported biscuits such as wafers, piroulines, petits-beurres, shortbreads	
	Assorted fruit slices such as plum, peach, banana, mango, starfruit	

1. Melt chocolate with Frangelico and water in the top of a double boiler set over (not in) hot water, for about 10 minutes.

2. Meanwhile, take your prettiest serving platter and decorate the edges with biscuits and fruits and 2 dainty forks. Leave a space in the middle for the chocolate.

3. Test the chocolate mixture by poking it with a fork: if it goes right through with no resistance, the chocolate is ready; if not, continue cooking for up to 5 minutes more. When the chocolate is extremely soft (miraculously, it still retains its shape), remove the double boiler from the heat. Using a fork or a small whisk, beat the chocolate for 1 to 2 minutes until all the liquids have been incorporated.

4. Transfer the chocolate to a beautiful bowl (crystal is best) and position at the center of your serving platter. Now you and your mate are free to cuddle up and dip fruit and biscuits into the chocolate.

Baked Peaches
with Almond Crust

SERVES 4

There is no more magical time of year than peach season. It's full summer, the peaches are juicy enough to gag you if you eat them too fast and the days are finally long enough to allow for leisurely, al fresco dinners, where waiting 20 minutes for dessert is actually a pleasure. The almond paste can be prepared in advance, but the peaches must be stuffed and baked to order, and served hot directly from the oven.

❋ ❋ ❋

PREHEAT OVEN TO 350°F (180°C)
BAKING DISH

6 tbsp	ground almonds	75 mL
2 tbsp	brown sugar or liquid honey or maple syrup	25 mL
1 tbsp	softened unsalted butter	15 mL
2	large ripe peaches (not cling type)	2
1 tsp	softened unsalted butter	5 mL
	Chocolate ice cream and/or raspberry coulis	

1. In a small bowl, combine ground almonds, sugar and 1 tbsp (15 mL) butter, mixing with a spoon to form a paste.

2. Cut a ring around the peaches and neatly separate them in halves. Remove pits. Lightly rub 1 tsp (5 mL) butter all over the peaches to grease the surfaces. Put peach halves in baking dish, skin-side down. Heap one-quarter of the almond paste into the pit cavity of each half.

3. Bake in preheated oven for 20 minutes. Serve (half a peach per portion) immediately, garnished with a dollop of ice cream and/or a smear of raspberry coulis.

Walnut Raisin Cake

MAKES 12 SLICES

Here's a butterless coffee cake that derives its moistness from raisins and its richness (as well as flavor) from ground walnuts. It is easy to put together — virtually failproof, with the only possible difficulty being that walnuts are one of the few nuts that are not sold pre-ground. The obvious solution is to buy walnut bits and grind them at home in a blender.

✳ ✳ ✳

Tip

If this cake seems a little chaste for your tastes, introduce some sinfulness by using the cake as the base for a slew of gooey, rich toppings such as melted chocolate, ice cream and fruit coulis. It also works splendidly toasted and buttered for tea time or breakfast.

PREHEAT OVEN TO 350°F (180°C)
10-INCH (4 L) TUBE PAN, OILED AND FLOURED

1 cup	all-purpose flour	250 mL
5	eggs	5
½ cup	granulated sugar	125 mL
1 tbsp	orange zest, finely chopped	15 mL
1¼ cups	ground walnuts (about 4 oz/125 g)	300 mL
1 cup	raisins	250 mL
1 tsp	baking powder	5 mL
⅓ cup	freshly squeezed orange juice	75 mL
	Confectioner's (icing) sugar, sifted	

1. Sift flour; set aside. In a large bowl, beat eggs, sugar and orange zest until frothy and canary yellow. Add walnuts, raisins and flour; do not mix. Sprinkle baking powder on top of the flour; pour orange juice on top of the powder to make it froth. Fold and beat ingredients lightly until incorporated into a thick, homogeneous batter.

2. Transfer into prepared cake pan. Tap it on the counter to settle, and bake in preheated oven for 40 minutes or until risen to twice its original height and cake tester comes out clean. Remove from oven. Let cake cool down completely.

3. Unmold cake by running a knife along both outer and inner walls of the ring. Invert onto a plate. Leave like that to highlight the bottom of the cake where most of the raisins will have descended. Garnish with sifted icing sugar to cover the surface and serve. Store, covered, at room temperature.

Greek Honey Cake

SERVES 12

Also known as revani, *this is the semolina-based cake with which Greeks amuse themselves when the baklava has run out. Easy to concoct — especially if your accomplishments include an acquaintance with beaten egg whites — this version is light and lively. It works spectacularly with serious dairy accompaniments, such as whipped cream, clotted cream or ice cream.*

Preheat oven to 350°F (180°C)
Deep 12-inch (30 cm) round cake pan, lightly oiled and dusted with flour

8	eggs, separated	8
½ cup	granulated sugar	125 mL
1 tbsp	finely chopped lemon zest	15 mL
1 cup	ground almonds	250 mL
½ cup	semolina	125 mL
1 tsp	baking powder	5 mL
3 tbsp	freshly squeezed lemon juice, divided	45 mL
1 cup	water	250 mL
1 cup	honey	250 mL

1. In a large bowl, beat egg yolks, sugar and lemon zest until pale yellow and thickened. Add ground almonds and semolina; do not mix. Sprinkle baking powder on top of semolina; pour 1 tbsp (15 mL) of the lemon juice on top of the powder to make it froth. Mix together just until combined.

2. In another bowl, beat egg whites until stiff. Stir about one-quarter of the egg whites into the batter. Add the rest of the egg whites and fold into the batter with circular motions from the bottom up, until mixed thoroughly but not deflated (do not beat).

3. Transfer to prepared cake pan. Bake in preheated oven for 30 minutes or until browned, risen to twice its original height and a cake tester comes out clean. Remove from oven; cool completely on a wire rack.

4. In a small saucepan, bring 1 cup (250 mL) water to a boil. Stir in honey and remaining lemon until dissolved. Return to a boil; reduce heat to medium and cook for 5 minutes, stirring occasionally. Pour hot syrup evenly over surface of cooled cake.

5. Let syrup absorb into the cake; cool once again. Do not unmold. Lift portions directly from the pan onto plates and serve either on its own or garnished with whipped cream or ice cream.

Almond Hazelnut Cake

SERVES 8

Almonds and hazelnuts are the two poles from which the world of European patisserie is suspended. These two flavorful nuts crop up in myriad guises throughout the sweet-tooth tapestry, which makes our lives ever so slightly more bearable. Here, they are used in tandem and perfumed with the orangey essence of Grand Marnier (or Cointreau or even a domestic Triple Sec).

Tip

Ground nuts are available in specialty and health stores and, often, even in supermarkets. If unlucky in finding both kinds of nuts, a full 1½ cups (375 mL) of either will do.

PREHEAT OVEN TO 350°F (180°C)
10-INCH (25 CM) PIE PLATE, LIGHTLY OILED AND DUSTED WITH FLOUR

¾ cup	ground almonds	175 mL
¾ cup	ground hazelnuts (see Tip, left)	175 mL
¼ cup	all-purpose flour	50 mL
¾ cup	granulated sugar	175 mL
½ cup	unsalted butter, melted	125 mL
3	eggs, beaten	3
¼ cup	Grand Marnier or other orange-flavored liqueur	50 mL
½ tsp	baking powder	2 mL
	Whipping (35%) cream and/or fruit coulis (optional)	

1. Put ground almonds and ground hazelnuts into a food processor. Sift flour right on the nuts. Add sugar and melted butter. Pulse a couple of times, then scrape down sides of bowl and process until well mixed and sticky. Add eggs and Grand Marnier; process until consistency is like very thick cream. Sprinkle with baking powder; pulse a few times until blended.
2. Transfer mixture to pie plate, tapping plate a couple of times to settle its contents. Bake in preheated oven for 35 to 40 minutes or until the top has browned, the sides have pulled in a little and cake tester comes out almost dry. Remove from oven and let cool down completely in the pie plate (the center will cave in very slightly). Serve wedges from the pie plate directly onto pools of the optional cream, with a light fruit coulis (peach, apricot, strawberry), or on its own.

National Library of Canada Cataloguing in Publication

Ayanoglu, Byron
 125 best vegetarian recipes / Byron Ayanoglu ; with contributions from Algis Kemezys.

Includes index.
ISBN 0-7788-0089-X

1. Vegetarian cookery. I. Kemezys, Algis II. Title. III. Title: One hundred twenty-five best vegetarian recipes.

TX837.A923 2004   641.5'636   C2003-906038-1

Index

❊ ❊ ❊